Cambridge El

Elements in Child Development
edited by
Marc H. Bornstein
National Institute of Child Health and Human Development, Bethesda
Institute for Fiscal Studies, London
UNICEF, New York City

WHOLE-CHILD DEVELOPMENT, LEARNING, AND THRIVING

A Dynamic Systems Approach

Pamela Cantor
Turnaround for Children
Richard M. Lerner
Tufts University
Karen J. Pittman
The Forum for Youth Investment
Paul A. Chase
Tufts University
Nora Gomperts
Turnaround for Children

CAMBRIDGE
UNIVERSITY PRESS

CAMBRIDGE
UNIVERSITY PRESS

University Printing House, Cambridge CB2 8BS, United Kingdom

One Liberty Plaza, 20th Floor, New York, NY 10006, USA

477 Williamstown Road, Port Melbourne, VIC 3207, Australia

314–321, 3rd Floor, Plot 3, Splendor Forum, Jasola District Centre,
New Delhi – 110025, India

79 Anson Road, #06–04/06, Singapore 079906

Cambridge University Press is part of the University of Cambridge.

It furthers the University's mission by disseminating knowledge in the pursuit of
education, learning, and research at the highest international levels of excellence.

www.cambridge.org
Information on this title: www.cambridge.org/9781108949569
DOI: 10.1017/9781108954600

First published 2021

A catalogue record for this publication is available from the British Library.

ISBN 978-1-108-94956-9 Paperback
ISSN 2632-9948 (online)
ISSN 2632-993X (print)

Additional resources for this publication at www.cambridge.org/whole-child

Whole-Child Development, Learning, and Thriving

A Dynamic Systems Approach

Elements in Child Development

DOI: 10.1017/9781108954600
First published online: April 2021

Pamela Cantor
Turnaround for Children

Richard M. Lerner
Tufts University

Karen J. Pittman
The Forum for Youth Investment

Paul A. Chase
Tufts University

Nora Gomperts
Turnaround for Children

Author for correspondence: Richard M. Lerner, Richard.Lerner@tufts.edu

Abstract: We discuss whole-child development, learning, and thriving through a dynamic systems theory lens that focuses on the United States and includes an analysis of historical challenges in the American public education system, including inequitable resources, opportunities, and outcomes. To transform US education systems, developmental and learning scientists, educators, policymakers, parents, and communities must apply the knowledge they have today to: (1) challenge the assumptions and goals that drove the design of the current US education system; (2) articulate a revised, comprehensive definition of whole-child development, learning, and thriving that accepts rather than simplifies how human beings develop; (3) create a profound paradigm shift in how the purpose of education is described in the context of social, cultural, and political forces, including the impacts of race, privilege, and bias; and (4) describe a new dynamic "language" for measurement of both the academic competencies and the full set of twenty-first century skills.

Keywords: whole-child development, learning, thriving, dynamic systems

ISBNs: 9781108949569 (PB), 9781108954600 (OC)
ISSNs: 2632-9948 (online), 2632-993X (print)

Contents

1 The Story We Will Tell

This Element explores and refines the concepts of whole-child development, learning, and thriving through a dynamic systems theory lens, integrating knowledge across multiple disciplines, including developmental and learning sciences. We provide a new, theory-predicated and evidence-based description of whole-child development, learning, and thriving (Lerner, 2018) and a vision for how to design learning environments that promote comprehensive, holistic, and equitable outcomes for all children.

We focus on the United States and begin by noting historical challenges in public education, including the intentional inequitable distribution of resources, opportunities, and outcomes that perpetuate racial and gender inequities. We discuss why earlier efforts to infuse whole-child development into US public schools have not produced the transformational change required to unleash the potential and unique capabilities of all students. We propose that to transform US education developmental and learning scientists, in full collaboration with educators, policymakers, and other key stakeholders (e.g., parents) (Bornstein, 2019a), must use their knowledge to: (1) challenge the assumptions that drove the design of current US education; (2) articulate a revised definition of whole-child development, learning, and thriving, (3) create a paradigm shift in how the purpose of education is described in the context of social, cultural, and political forces, including the impacts of racism, ethnicity, socioeconomic privilege, and bias; and (4) introduce a dynamic "language" for measuring the full set of twenty-first century skills and mastery-level academic competencies.

Our story begins with a review of key concepts from developmental and learning sciences and dynamic systems theory. Next, we call for a twenty-first century education system that embraces the nature of human development and learning as part of an integrated and dynamic system of relations between individual and context (including, most superordinate, culture) (Immordino-Yang et al., 2019; Raeff, 2016). We explain that this system promotes design, practice, and measurement approaches optimizing opportunities for development, learning, and thriving for all children in all settings in which children grow and learn. The final sections of the Element offer a *blueprint* for practice with examples of organizations that have designed settings, programs, and tools to operationalize the principles set forth in this Element. We review research on the characteristics of settings that promote whole-child development, learning, and thriving and propose a framework to influence school design, educator practice, measurement, and policy. We conclude with a discussion of the impact of the contexts facing children, their families, and our learning systems as of January 2021 (the time of writing), considering the combined effects of

COVID-19, racialized violence, and economic instability, all of which dispro-
portionately impact communities of color.

1.1 Conceptions of Whole-Child Development

"Whole-child development" can mean many different things to educators,
researchers, foundations, and policymakers. Whole-child development has
been referred to as: (1) a collaborative approach to integrating health services
and programs more deeply into the day-to-day life of schools to ensure that all
students are healthy, safe, engaged, supported, and challenged (Lewallen et al.,
2015); (2) explicit social and emotional learning (SEL) instruction and integration of social, emotional, and academic skills development (Brackett et al.,
2015); and (3) a comprehensive approach to children that builds on the understanding that physical conditions, emotional states, and social experiences (i.e.,
relationships) have a direct impact on learning and that student success and
well-being must be conceptualized and measured to include more than academic skills and knowledge acquisition (e.g., Jones & Kahn, 2017). Each of
these views of whole-child development is based on research and evidence.
Each was created to challenge the status quo of US education, resulting in
a plethora of policy standards, program offerings, and partnership models (e.g.,
wraparound student services, SEL curricula, community schools, whole-school
transformation models). As we shall explain, these viewpoints are incomplete
and do not address the holist, dynamics, and specificity of child development
(Bornstein, 2019b; Rose, 2016).

Although these frameworks represent significant and important progress,
none fully addresses the heart of the problem facing US education: Schools
were designed based on incorrect (and often racist) assumptions about how
children learn and develop. Current US education systems have been designed
in a context of white supremacy, ethnocentrism, and a focus on certification,
socialization, and social control (e.g., Fass, 1991; Payne, 1984; Tucker, 2020a,
2020b). Past approaches to whole-child development and associated programs
and policies failed to address incorrect assumptions or the influence of racism
on the design of schools. They were also not fully informed by (1) biological,
social, behavioral, and social science research or (2) methodological innovations in measurement and data analysis. Together, these bodies of research and
methods of analysis affirm that child development (and human development in
general) involves a system of "dynamic" (i.e., mutually influential) relations
among:

(1) each child's multiple biological processes (e.g., the nervous system and
    epigenetic influences on the developing brain);

(2) each child's psychological processes (cognitive, affective, and behavioral) and social relational processes; and

(3) the collective set of coactive ecological and cultural contexts that each child encounters across the life span, ranging from proximal child–parent/family relationships to more distal contexts of schools and communities, to macro contexts involving societal institutions, culture, race, ethnicity, the natural and designed physical ecology, and histories (Bornstein, 2019a; Bronfenbrenner & Morris, 2006).

In this Element, we propose that a comprehensive understanding of whole-child development, learning, and thriving requires *a dynamic and integrated view of each child's journey*. Current scientific understanding of these dynamic, individualized journeys must become the foundation for the beliefs and practices of practitioners, administrators, and policymakers. Specifically, practitioners, administrators, and policymakers must understand the learning processes, potentialities, and capabilities that can and will emerge in students across time and across dynamically coactive settings designed to promote whole-child development, learning, and thriving.

1.2 Thriving and Resilience

Thriving is a dynamic process that goes beyond well-being to include individual growth that is strength-based and multidimensional, reflecting positive growth across multiple domains including physical, emotional, and cognitive. These domains are linked to internal processes and external conditions that enable favorable change (Slavich & Cole, 2013). Thriving involves a child's holistic, adaptive behavior and development that is, and can be, optimized during specific times in life and in specific community and cultural settings (Lerner, 2004).

Masten (2014b) discussed the concept of thriving and differentiated it from resilience, defining resilience as "the capacity of a dynamic system to adapt successively to disturbances that threaten system function, viability, or development" (p. 1012). She explained that this definition was intended to be "scalable across systems and disciplines, from the level of micro-organisms and systems operating within the human organism to the system of family, school, community, culture, economy, society, or climate" (p. 1012). Masten (2014b) was prescient in noting that a key reason for using this broad, dynamic systems-based orientation to resilience sprang from increasing international concern with integrating diverse scientific fields to comprehensively address problems that are based in interdependent systems of function and recovery. Masten's vision is certainly relevant to the present authors, who wrote this

Element in the context of the COVID-19 pandemic and a period of heightened awareness of racialized violence and resulting civil unrest (see Section 7).

In distinguishing between thriving and resilience, Masten (2014b) noted that scholars studying thriving (Lerner, 2004) or positive youth development (PYD) (e.g., Lerner et al., 2015) conceptualize both resilience and thriving as involving dynamic, mutually influential relations between specific children and their contexts (youth⇔context relations). Moreover, both resilience and thriving involve "positive aspects of development, function, resources, and strengths, both in the individual and in the context" (Masten, 2014b, p. 1013). However, Masten (2014b) saw resilience as a subset of child⇔context relations located at the high end of a continuum of risk or adversity. Therefore, to both Masten (2014b) and the present authors, resilience is not a person or a context phenomenon; like thriving, resilience is a person⇔context relational phenomenon. Resilience is, then, an instance of adaptive functioning in high risk or adverse settings.

The concepts of thriving and resilience require attention to children's positive adaptation to the specific features of their context. However, thriving focuses on optimal functioning, whereas resilience attends to adequate or "okay" functioning, largely because resilience research has focused on children and families facing enormous challenges, adversity, or trauma (e.g., see Masten, 2007, 2014a; Masten et al., 2015). We agree, then, with Osher, Pittman, et al. (2020) that thriving is a dynamic process of optimal learning and development, and that "Thriving is influenced by individual and community assets, one's own sense of agency (i.e., belief in one's ability to achieve), and connection to the world. Thriving is informed by and informs collective and individual meaning-making. Thriving is grounded in one's beliefs and values" (p. 3). David Osher elaborates his views about thriving in Box 1.

Accordingly, in this Element we focus on thriving because we believe that our approach to whole-child development enables programs and policies to promote positive and healthy development, including for children who have experienced significant adversity and oppression. We propose that this knowledge be linked to policy and design recommendations and to adopting a different world view of twenty-first century education – one involving dynamic systems (versus fixed determinism). This world view would allow us to embrace the complexity of learning, development, and thriving rather than working to oversimplify them.

1.3 Historical and False Assumptions in Public Education

Public education in the United States was designed based on a set of false assumptions and without a comprehensive understanding or knowledge of

David Osher

Equity and thriving have been matters of policy and intellectual concern during the last two decades, but they are often discussed without reference to institutionalized racism and privilege. The social, emotional, physical, and economic effects of the COVID-19 pandemic, and their relation to and amplification of preexisting disparities have raised the salience of equity and thriving. The salience of these issues has been deepened by the increased visibility of state-sanctioned racist and ethnocentric violence and by palpable manifestations of the historical and ecological determinants of inequity and ill-being (Osher, Pittman, et al., 2020). George Floyd's murder by police officers carrying out routinized behavior is a highly visible illustration of the experience of people of color almost since the first Europeans arrived in North America (Hinton et al., 2014; Takaki, 2012). Police ignoring of his statements regarding his health conditions, including his pleas that he could not breathe, embody an unwillingness to listen to those whom we "other" or fear as well as a willingness to ignore their fundamental humanity.

Although the concern for equity and thriving has been amplified, we need approaches to equity and thriving that are responsive to the perceptions, needs, and voices of groups that have been marginalized and minoritized – groups that have been subject to victim-blaming social policies that are justified by hegemonic thinking that reflects siloed and reductionist approaches, along with the institutionalization and mystification of privilege. New approaches to equity and thriving must address the historical nestedness and dynamic nature of thriving, including dynamically related biological, phenomenological, and social processes that contribute to thriving (Osher, Pittman, et al., 2020).

Equity has often been conceptualized and operationalized in a siloed, static, formalist, culturally narrow, and minimalist manner. Although these minimalist approaches may open some socially created gates, they do not open them far enough. Test performance may still be a gatekeeper, but high-stakes tests do not measure attainment over time; measuring a narrow set of attributes at one time in one context does not measure readiness for life or make it likely that individuals will have the capacity to realize a meaningful and healthy life.

Perhaps more important, approaches to equity and thriving driven by minimalist standards do not provide learners with a means to address institutionalized racism and privilege – they neither enable individuals to fully address opportunity structures that are stacked against them nor do they prepare individuals to work with others to change the conditions that affect them. For example, eliminating formal bias (say, to enrichment opportunities) does not eliminate informal and sometimes less visible barriers (e.g., microaggressions, stereotype threat, and acculturative stress). The success of any individual in overcoming these obstacles does not eliminate the impacts of the need to address oppression or eliminate socially constructed hurdles that others will face. A richer approach to equity includes universal access to opportunities to develop attributes that contribute not only to well-being, but dynamically to individual and collective thriving – socially, emotionally, physically, cognitively, spiritually, and economically – in coacting dimensions that collectively foster thriving. As the COVID-19 pandemic and the Black Lives Matter movement vividly illustrate, thriving cannot just be individual. Our capacity to thrive, particularly over time, is dynamically linked to the well-being of others. This relation includes our proximal environment, those who support us, or with whom we affiliate, live, or work, the other living beings on the planet, and the health of our globe.

developmental and learning science. Table 1 presents these false assumptions about whole-child development, learning, and thriving and the information needed to correct mistakes derived from these assumptions. Specifically, formal education was designed without recognizing the integrated, dynamic, and individual nature of human development that undergirds the learning process itself. Across states, public education focused on delivery and acquisition of content – primarily math and English – using standardized approaches that presume a bell

Table 1 False assumptions and correct information about whole-child development, learning, and thriving

False assumptions	Knowledge and evidence
1. Genes are the primary determinant of learning and development (rather than context). Contexts and relationships (in school and outside) are secondary contributors to skill development and mastery of content. Intelligence and cognitive abilities are fixed, and personality is stable. (This view is a genetic reductionist assumption.)	1. Contexts – relationships, environments, and experiences in and out of school – are the primary determinants of learning and development (e.g., Immordino-Yang et al., 2019; Slavich, 2020).
2. Talent and skills are scarce, distributed in a bell curve. Specific students (in too many cases, white or middle- and upper-class white boys) have talent and skills (determined by genes); others (in far too many cases, students of color, poor students, and girls) do not. The system should be designed to identify and support those with purported innate talent and skills.	2. Talents and skills are ubiquitous. Education should be designed to reveal the talents and skills in each child (Bloom, 1985; Bornstein & Putnick, 2019; Csikszentmihalyi et al., 1993).
3. An average score on a test usually administered once a year represents a student's competency and is a good enough approximation of what the student knows. Measuring an average score is sufficient for understanding the competency of individuals.	3. There is no such thing as an average child; an average of anything rarely represents any attribute of the individuals being measured in the average (Molenaar, 2007; Rose, 2016).
4. Memorization of content and facts will lead to mastery, competence, and higher-order thinking skills. Measurement of content acquisition is a good representation of student competency.	4. Mastery of content, competence, and higher-order thinking skills come when educators scaffold and teach essential skills and engage each child with challenging, relevant content within the child's zone of proximal development during each period of development, to accomplish mastery of multiple competencies (Vygotsky, 1978).

Table 1 (cont.)

False assumptions	Knowledge and evidence
5. The potential of a student as a learner is knowable in advance; some children arrive at school ready to engage in learning (especially white, middle- and upper-socioeconomic status children), and others (especially lower socioeconomic status and children of color) do not. Skill and competency development are discrete, linear, and measurable. Growth trajectories are predictable.	5. The potential of a child is not knowable in advance. The purpose of education should be to develop and extend the talents and potential in each child. Human development is a jagged process with peaks and valleys along the way (Rose, 2016).
6. Student agency and beliefs about intelligence are not relevant to identity formation and require adjustments in expectations and opportunities by leaders and teachers. Specifically, children of color are assumed to be growing up in poverty, ill-suited to educational settings and academic rigor, and even prone to criminality.	6. Student agency and student and teacher beliefs about intelligence are highly relevant to identity formation (Dweck, 2016).
7. Adversity does not disrupt learning or developmental processes.	7. Adversity can have effects on the neural systems that govern learning and behavior, but with support from caring, trusted adults, these effects are preventable and reversible; children can overcome the effects of adversity and thrive (McEwen, 2013; Slavich, 2020; Slavich & Cole, 2013).

curve of abilities and talents, with most children falling in the middle of the distribution. The systems have not responded to the variation in how students learn by using more personalized approaches or by developing crucial twenty-first century metacognitive and deeper learning skills (Bornstein & Putnick, 2019). They were not designed to intentionally develop the learner or to promote equity; they were designed to offer access to rich learning opportunities to specific groups but not to marginalized groups based on race, gender, and culture (Raeff, 2016). Indeed, Osher, Pittman, et al. (2020) and Tucker (2020a, 2020b) noted that the US education system was designed to select and sort, and that institutionalized racism, classism, and segregation remain embedded in this system. Although space limitations preclude our discussing this history of US education and its contemporary (at this writing) manifestations, interested readers may consult several reviews documenting these points (see Farrington, 2020; Nasir et al., 2020; Okonofua et al., 2016; Wilkerson, 2020; Winthrop, 2018) and, several of the Boxes included in this Element.

The reviews we have noted document how the failure to address inequitable funding, opportunities, and outcomes result from persistent systems of institutional and individual oppression in US schools and communities (e.g., racial, ethnic, and gender stereotypes, fixed mindsets, historical inequities in opportunities for deeper learning). Failure also derives from an unwillingness to address and eliminate inaccurate and unchecked assumptions about how children learn, develop, and respond to adversity and opportunity. Finally, failure derives from underestimating or ignoring the power and potential of individuals and systems to enhance life and academic outcomes, perhaps most importantly for children who have experienced adversity and stress over extended periods. Researchers, educators, and policymakers should understand individual children's specific sensitivities to the effects of cumulative stress, or allostatic load (McEwen, 2013), associated with specific inequities of socioeconomic and relational resources available in their specific contexts, and to the stresses experienced by their caregivers, family members, teachers, and child workers (e.g., Laceulle et al., 2019; Osher, Cantor, et al., 2020). For instance, McEwen (2013) noted that:

> The brain, itself, is also a target of stress and stress-related hormones and it undergoes structural and functional remodeling and significant changes in gene expression that are adaptive under normal circumstances but which can lead to damage when stress is excessive. The growing recognition of the adaptive plasticity and stress vulnerability of the brain itself, beginning with the hippocampus, now includes other brain regions such as the amygdala and prefrontal cortex and fear related memories, working memory, and self-regulatory behaviors. The interactions between these brain regions during the biological embedding of experiences over the life course determines whether events in the social and physical environment will lead to successful adaptation or to maladaptation and impaired mental and physical health, with implications for understanding health disparities and the impact of early life adversity and for intervention and prevention strategies. (p. 673)

As we begin to discuss in the next portion of this section, US education and the experience it produces for students would be very different if it directly addressed institutionalized racism, privilege, and bias and used foundational knowledge from developmental and learning sciences (e.g., Bailey et al., 2019). Understanding how to influence learning and developmental processes in learning settings, both formal and informal (i.e., in out-of-school-time, youth development programs) (Lerner et al., 2015), will help to create a different educational reality with substantially better outcomes for many more children.

1.4 The Science of Learning and Development

There is burgeoning scientific knowledge about the biologic systems that govern human life, including the systems of the human brain. Today, researchers can study the brain's structure, wiring, metabolism, and connections to other systems of the body and to the external world (Immordino-Yang et al., 2019). This work underscores the "nurture of nature" by documenting a new understanding of the deep interdependence of biological and sociocultural processes in the growth of the brain (Immordino-Yang et al., 2019). Researchers know much more than they did when twentieth century US public education was designed. It is the responsibility of all people interested in children's thriving to use this knowledge to design a system characterized by *robust* equity (Osher, Pittman, et al., 2020, p. 3).

When thinking about how to apply new science to reshape the US education system, it is helpful to consider fields such as medicine. What was done when researchers learned that germs – not miasma – cause disease? When we learned that cancers can be transmitted, not like infections, but instead through gene mutations? Although health disparities continue to exist, there have been dramatic changes in medicine in the last fifty years based on new knowledge – cures for diseases, changes in how scientists conduct research, and changes in how physicians practice medicine, in part because of a willingness to challenge assumptions and build new knowledge. Unfortunately, the same willingness to challenge assumptions and the magnitude of advances have not happened in US public education.

To apply the new knowledge of human development and learning, developmental and learning researchers, educators, and policymakers must: (1) challenge the assumptions and goals that serve as the foundation for current US public education; (2) articulate and popularize a revised conception of whole-child development, learning, and thriving so that these are the norm across educational settings; (3) accept – rather than seek to simplify – the complexities in how humans develop; and (4) create a profound paradigm shift in how the purpose of education is described and enacted by educators, in communities, and among policymakers.

In Section 2, we present the key concepts from developmental science, learning science, and dynamic systems theories that support a new, bold purpose for twenty-first century education. These concepts and principles challenge the false assumptions that drove the design of the current US education system and present what is known today about how children learn and develop. These ideas should serve as the foundation for a twenty-first century education that reveals and develops the potential of every child.

2 Key Concepts: Dynamic Systems Theory, Developmental Science, and Learning Science

There is no separation of nature and nurture, biology and environment, or brain and behavior, but only a collaborative coordination between them.

K. Fischer & T. Bidell (2006, p. 383)

No living organism comes into being independent of another living organism (Tobach & Schneirla, 1968). Therefore, to understand fully the biology of any organism, its relationships to other organisms must be understood. Among humans, the first and most important relationship is between parent and offspring, which provides foundational sources of healthy physiological, psychological, and behavioral development (Bornstein, 2019a). From the very beginning of human life and across the life span, there are fundamental links among biological, psychological, behavioral, and social functioning (e.g., Gottlieb, 1998).

An embryo is an extraordinary feat of human development, a structure composed of multiple substructures, with every future system that a human being will have or need represented as well as the potential for mutually influential connections and integration between the embryo and all of the other levels of organization involved in human life. The embryo is, then, a pluripotential structure that provides a powerful example of dynamic theories of human development. In fact, the embryo will be both the metaphor and lens through which we represent the structural sequences and processes that produce a whole human being, including the activation of those processes through experiences and relationships that bring a human being fully to life across the life span.

This developmental process, termed *probabilistic epigenesis*, is one of the central features of dynamic systems theory (Gottlieb, 1998; see too Fischer & Bidell, 2006). We present this conception of development in this Element – the pluripotentiality of each and every human being – recognizing the scholarly base in embryology and dynamic systems from which it is derived and with the hope that this body of science can provide a strong foundation for promoting healthy and positive development, learning, equity, and social justice for all children (Immordino-Yang et al., 2019; Lee, 2010; Spencer, 2006).

The dynamic systems model of development, learning, and thriving reflects a world view that may be illustrated by the mathematics of nonlinear dynamics, complexity theory, and quantum mechanics. Reference to this illustration enables us to contrast the worldview of Newtonian physics, which conceptualizes the universe as a uniform and fixed entity involving fixed determinism, with a worldview, found in quantum mechanics, of a universe that varies across time and place (Zukav, 1979; see too Bornstein, 2019b; Elder et al., 2015; Overton, 2015).

The individual elements of the universe change in ways that cannot be fully predicted in advance, because *relationships* among elements determine change, and these relationships vary based on the time and place in which they occur. Therefore, fixed deterministic laws about the elements of the universe are replaced by probabilistic laws (Zukav, 1979). Although the math of Newtonian physics is verifiable and useful for macro facets of the universe (e.g., the equation for Newton's law of universal gravitation), it is not useful for understanding the course of change – the life span of molecular, individual components of the universe. In the world view of quantum mechanics, the individual must be understood through the perspective of multidimensional change over time, the effects of time-specific relationships, and the effects of other specific components of their context.

Probability, not fixity, within a system in which all elements are integrated is the world view of quantum mechanics (Zukav, 1979) *and* of the scholarship that frames a dynamic science of learning and development (e.g., Bornstein, 2019b; Overton, 2015). The US education community – including researchers and scholars of learning science – has not yet applied a dynamic systems theory approach and the comprehensive integration of essential elements it could generate to the design of US education systems. The current disruptions caused by the combined effects of the COVID-19 pandemic, racial violence and social unrest, and economic instability may be a force powerful enough to bring about this transformation.

Medicine, however, has already had to embrace this kind of approach. Physicians know that they cannot treat a kidney, heart disease, or cancer as if a malady is an isolated problem that can be addressed without understanding the conditions of the organs, the patient's family history, gender, lifestyle, ethnicity, socioeconomic status and life situations, and proclivity to follow physician advice. Holistic medicine is not an optional approach to human health; rather, it is a requirement of modern medical practice (Halfon & Forrest, 2018). The *system of relationships* among cells, tissues, and organs, and their relations with the world surrounding the person, must be understood because *mutually influential relationships* (i.e., *dynamic relationships*) connect all parts of the system (Halfon et al., 2018; Slavich & Cole, 2013). From the genetic to the social and cultural, human development across the life span involves *a dynamic, fully integrated system* (Jablonka & Lamb, 2005; Slavich & Cole, 2013). In fact, this is the story of evolution itself – an expansive and expanded story of inheritance that exists across generations, operating beyond the level of the gene, and absorbing the forces that drive gene expression, in particular, the context of each human life.

Scholars working in the fields of developmental and learning science and educational research and practice are beginning to appreciate the necessity of *a holistic approach to learning, thriving, and development* (Cantor et al., 2019; Osher, Cantor, et al., 2020). Focusing alone on the cognitive facets of achievements in language, mathematics, or science is insufficient because context – relationships, environments, and experiences – provides the energy that drives the brain's electrical circuitry and develops the neural pathways that build increasingly complex skills. This energy flow drives the connections between brain structures that produce the development of all complex skills (e.g., reading, writing), especially complex cognitive skills (Fischer & Bidell, 2006; Mascolo & Fischer, 2015). Relationships are the precursors for learner engagement, competency development, and mastery of domain-specific knowledge, motivation, higher-order problem-solving skills, and ultimately, academic achievement (Baltes et al., 2006).

Adverse experiences occur both inside and out of school. Such experiences will influence a child's thoughts, feelings, behaviors, and attainments in any learning setting. Disparities in opportunities and marginalization based on race, ethnicity, gender, religion, community, access, etc. can enhance or thwart chances for thriving (Sampson, 2016), both in and out of school. In turn, belief in one's ability to grow, learn, and succeed through education – both in and out of the classroom – may be more important than any specific curriculum for predicting and nurturing educational outcomes and life successes. Unfortunately for marginalized students, this belief is shaped significantly by class-based ethnic and gender stereotypes and discriminatory practices. In short, multiple factors influence a child's growth and development, for good or for bad.

Context – positive and negative – drives human development and, more specifically, brain development (Immordino-Yang et al., 2019); accordingly, to understand and enhance the healthy development and the lifelong learning skills of each child (Immordino-Yang & Knecht, 2020), developmental scientists and education curriculum developers must embrace a holistic and dynamic systems-based approach. This approach will allow them to specify the elements of an integrated design to support twenty-first century learning based in twenty-first century science and directed toward equity of experience and opportunity.

In his 1984 "2 Sigma" paper, Bloom argued that what one child can do, nearly all children can do under highly favorable conditions. This statement should force educators to recognize that the purpose of the twenty-first century education system must be to define and establish those "highly favorable conditions" – conditions that develop productive and engaged learners, promote the acquisition of complex and adaptive skills, and drive academic growth from any developmental starting point toward a diversity of possible educational outcomes. For example, such diverse outcomes include dispositions toward thinking and learning based on either child-defined and child-specific goals or the goals of others (e.g., specific educators) (see Immordino-Yang & Knecht, 2020).

2.1 Specific Developmental Principles and Their Relations to Individuality, Complexity, and the Emerging Competencies of Children

Dynamic systems theories explain that children – and all individuals – are in dynamic relations with the worlds around them from the time they are in utero (e.g., Csikszentmihalyi & Rathunde, 1998; Freedle, 1977; Thelen & Smith, 2006). These dynamic relations influence the development of the body and the mind. They help explain the notoriously spontaneous, unpredictable, and creative nature of human beings (Boldrini et al., 1998).

The human brain is an elaborate, complex system that follows the laws of nonlinear dynamics, one property of which is its ability to self-organize in adaptive or maladaptive ways in response to openness or constraints of experience (Schore, 2016; Siegel, 2020). Self-organization of the brain means that the person, as a complex living system, will build and organize skills to attain goals. Those goals may be adaptive for survival or evolve to solve a specific problem using increasingly complex skills (Fischer & Bidell, 2006; Mascolo & Fischer, 2015). The processing power of the brain, through the pathways of billions of neurons, yields a unique ability of the person to remember, compare, and generalize across experiences.

One feature of development involves changes in the strength of synaptic connections. Although the capacity for synaptic strength can be encoded in DNA, a far more powerful determinant of synaptic strength, leading to the development of complex skills, is derived from the consistent firing and patterns of firing of neurons that are the products of our experiences. As reflected in Hebb's (1949, 1955) axiom that neurons that fire together become wired together, such coaction produces more deeply engrained pathways. The probability of activation of such pathways increases as neurons and groups of neurons fire together, thereby leading to the development of more complex skills. These skills will be determined by history, present experiences, and current environmental conditions, either positive or negative. Post and Weiss (1997) provided a developmental perspective to Hebb's axiom, noting that neurons that fire together both survive and wire together. Such circuits developed in early periods of life can form the functional basis for enduring patterns later on in life (Immordino-Yang & Damasio, 2007; Siegel, 2020).

In their seminal work on dynamic system theory, Fischer and Bidell (2006) explained:

> Skills do not spring up fully grown from preformed rules or logical structures. They are built up gradually through the practice of real activities in real contexts, and they are gradually extended to new contexts through this same constructive process . . .. A skill draws on and unites systems for emotion, memory, planning, communication, cultural and historical scripts, speech, gesture, and so forth. Each of these systems must work in concert with the others for an individual to tell an organized story or perform a complex task in a way that it will be understood and appreciated. The concept of dynamic skill facilitates the study of relations among collaborating systems and the patterns of variation they produce and inhibits treating psychological processes as isolated modules that obscure relations among cooperating systems. (p. 321)

And further that:

> Skills are context-specific and culturally defined. Real mental and physical activities are organized to perform specific functions, in particular settings . . .. The context specificity of skills is related to the characteristics of integration and inter-participation because people build skills to participate with other people directly in specific contexts for particular sociocultural and adaptive reasons. And, as a result, skills take on a cultural patterning. (p. 322)

Integrating the principle of specificity (Bornstein, 2017, 2019b) with a rejection of a focus on aggregate or average depictions of a child (Molenaar & Nesselroade, 2015; Rose, 2016), Fischer and Bidell (2006) argued that ideas about how to enhance a child's specific pathway through the educational system and across life should begin with an analysis of the role of context, include an appreciation of the fact that variability is fundamental to human action, and that humans vary their actions in order to enact skilled performance. Fischer and Bidell believed that person-in-context and variability-as-information are the fundamental principles of dynamic systems theory.

In summary, dynamic skills link active children in a dynamic relation with their changing world at multiple levels of organization. The constructive nature of these relations means that any facet of a specific child's web of experience is potentially malleable and can alter the strength of synaptic connections

influencing the organizing of the brain, the patterning of complex skill formation, and the increasingly adaptive nature of skill development, *if* contextual
influences enable them. This fact alone means that inequities of experience
based on race, social class, gender, ethnicity, religion, ability status, or sexual
orientation (which, as a group, may be referred to as systemic societal inequities) are not biologically mandated necessities of nature. They are disparities
that exist based on false beliefs, prejudices, or oppressive policies established
by privileged groups (Lee, 2010; Spencer, 2006). When such systemic societal
inequities are addressed, the malleability of human beings to positive experiences and relationships can unfold.

What follows is an application of the key concepts in dynamic systems and
nonlinear dynamics to the unfolding story of how an embryo becomes a human
being. The concepts are ordered to account for the beginning – the embodied
nature of the embryo itself and the human being it will become. We discuss the
opportunities and constraints in the experiences and environments the embryo is
exposed to and the intimate microprocesses through which developmental
opportunity and intention get expressed. We point to the emergence of novelty
and to how the systems of body and mind move from simplicity toward
increasing complexity, adaptation, and stability.

2.1.1 Embodiment

The human body has biological components. In addition, it carries a history of
specific experiences (the body as a psychological entity). The body is also an
entity that is actively engaged with the specific world within which it lives (the
body as a sociocultural entity) (Overton, 2015). Accordingly, there is no such
thing as a mental process lodged exclusively inside the brain that directs the
development of a human being. A human being is a living complex system
composed of subsystems that connect the molecular to the cellular, cellular to
the organ, organs to the person, and the person to the sociocultural and physical
ecological levels of the system. Embodiment depicts the ongoing coaction
between these systems and levels, internal and external, and conveys the
interpenetrating and bidirectional nature of experience at every level of the
development of a human being (Immordino-Yang & Yang, 2017).

Experience is not additive; rather, it is transformational through the process of
embodiment, which occurs through positive and negative feedback loops
between a specific individual and specific contexts, and involves changes marked
by increasing differentiation, integration, and complexity of skill development.
The specific life pathway of a child involves specific embodying experiences, that
is specific individual⇔context relations (Overton, 2015; Rose, 2016).

Current educational systems were not designed to support the coactions represented by the concept of embodiment. For example, a singular focus on the cognitive components of achievements in language, mathematics, or science is insufficient because social, emotional, affective, and relational development shape intellectual growth and learning (Immordino-Yang et al., 2019). Devotion to a narrow, content-oriented learning process alone – at the exclusion of these other facets of holistic development – provides an incomplete understanding of the processes that shape the specific attributes of a child.

2.1.2 Context

Contexts include the environments, experiences, and relationships in a human life. Context is composed of levels of organization within each person's body: genes, cells, organs, systems (e.g., nervous, circulatory, digestive, and respiratory) and the chemicals circulating within and across these physiological levels. Context also includes the levels of the person's social, cultural, and physical world within which the person is embedded (social relationships, neighborhoods and communities, social institutions, the physical ecology, and culture). Within a dynamic systems approach to human development, all levels of context are integrated, relational, bidirectional, and coactive. As such, context drives our biology and our genetics, with each person's life course shaped by the specific features of these levels as they coact with a human being across time and place.

For example, traumatic events can impact the developmental systems of children – their biology, behavior, learning, and social relationships. Trauma itself is a disruption to development that is agnostic to the event. Trauma produces alterations in mood, focus, concentration, memory, behavior, emotions, and trust. Failures to interrogate the role of context in contributing to trauma and developmental inequities are discussed by Margaret Beale Spencer in Box 2.

2.1.3 Cultural Embeddedness

Culture frames the way individuals construct and convey meaning about every facet of their lives, including their specific history of individual⇔context relations. Culture is a set of dynamic processes, not a fixed or monolithic entity. Culture functions as a system of dynamic meanings, practices, values, and artifacts, and culture varies from family to family, by geography, socioeconomic status, race, language, and nation of origin (Jablonka & Lamb, 2005; Raeff, 2016).

The biology of humans coacts with the specific, culturally shaped contexts within which humans develop to create specific expressions of human attributes

BOX 2 INTERROGATING THE DEVELOPMENTAL CONTEXT OF "WE THE PEOPLE"

Margaret Beale Spencer

A major accomplishment awaiting "normalization" in the social sciences – with special significance for developmental scholarship – is the incorporation of context. References to an implied awareness of *the ecology of human development* are often present, but the delineation of *how the system of dynamic forces intersect with human development processes* remains infrequent. The absence is consequential for a nation of diverse citizens representing varied historical circumstances. The short-coming matters deeply and scaffolds the *unavoidability of human vulnerability in twenty-first century America* (i.e., the balance [or imbalance]) between risks and assets (Spencer, 2008).

For the nation's diverse children (e.g., class, ethnicity, immigration status, gender), *making sense of circumstances and responding with patterned coping to normative and nonnormative human development tasks matters* and provides important policy and practice developmental science insights (e.g., social, health, educational, and justice). We posit that *all humans maintain a level of unavoidable vulnerability* (Spencer, 2006), involving patchy and varied coverage due to privileges, the character and depth of risks and challenges confronted, and associated experiences (or lack thereof). Accordingly, there is potential for a "downside of privilege" as well as for "resiliency outcomes."

Traditionally unacknowledged, the historical or chronosystem level of the ecology (Bronfenbrenner & Morris, 2006) introduces significant risk for US children. The tradition to ignore the nation's 400 years of history particularly compromises developmental science. For example, research practices focus on human development processes for privileged children, and at the same time, highlight, devalue, and stigmatize untoward outcomes as the focus for racially and socially devalued youngsters. The under-interrogated US Constitution "We the People" social self-identifier encourages the resistance to history that delineates contextual features including the mistreatment of groups of people. The shortcoming scaffolds and undermines the daily lives of the nation's distinctive groups and identifies sources of balance or imbalance between risks and assets (i.e., human vulnerability) as individuals navigate social spaces.

Condoleezza Rice, as the sixty-sixth United States Secretary of State and the twentieth United States National Security Advisor, framed the shortcoming distinctively as *America's birth defect*; being a person of color matters. Creating the analogy of starting out as a tiny flaw in a home's structure and growing over time, Isabel Wilkerson (2020) characterized inattentiveness to historical context as a flaw. She defined the situation and salience as that of *caste*. As a critical component of the ecology of human development, ignored history functions as an indelible aspect of the US context, which differentially influences individuals' life chances and vulnerability level. For scientific best practice, *context acknowledgment* increases innovation; its incorporation decreases static representations of experiences to ones which appreciate variability in coping processes and impact. It provides opportunities for modeled and trained practices and policies and programs that afford authentic sources of supports and opportunities. In sum, it diminishes misguided assumptions about exceptionalism and delivers opportunities for the experience of genuine assets and access to authentic opportunities intended by constitutional reference to "We the People."

that vary across cultural communities. Examples of biological⇔cultural coactional processes include: the nature of attachment and family relationships; conceptions of one's identity; the meaning of thriving within one's community; processes of learning; and the patterns of meaning humans apply to prior experiences, including experiences relating to poverty, racism, and social disparities (McAdoo, 1999; McLoyd et al., 2015; Murry et al., 2015; Nasir et al., 2014; Raeff, 2016; Spencer, 2006; Spencer et al., 2015).

Thus, human cultural variation represents patterns of adaptation to and/or coping with specific environments through multiple pathways that offer models of both risk and resilience (e.g., Masten et al., 2015; Spencer, 2006; Spencer et al., 2015). Many ecological factors come together dynamically to influence the processes of human learning, adaptation, and development. The manifestation of these processes, which are also linked biologically, shape our experiences in the world and the meanings we attribute to them (Lee, 2010). Thinking, feeling, and perceiving, derived from the embeddedness of culture in home-school-community-peer social networks, constitute a dynamic system with self-organizing properties (Lee et al., 2020; Nasir et al., 2014). Na'ilah Suad Nasir provides additional discussion in Box 3 of the role of culture and race in learning.

A key illustration of the role of culture in the learning and development of children is provided by Fischer and Bidell (2006), who discussed cultural embeddedness as part of the acquisition of dynamic, complex skills. They emphasized the context specificity and cultural embeddedness of all skills. Their central point is that individuals will develop skills to coact effectively with the specific social, physical, and cultural context they encounter at specific times in their lives.

Culture is exemplified by one of its tools – language (Jablonka & Lamb, 2005; Mistry & Dutta, 2015). Language is a rule-governed system of signs that is constructed by the child through developmentally specific coactions with the specific uses of the word available in the child's culture and comprehensible within the child's developmental range. The specific meanings of the word to a specific child arise through specific exchanges with the symbol system in the child's family, community, and cultural setting as the child coacts with the people and artifacts of the culture at specific points in life.

Cognitive processes involved in the use of conceptual tools demonstrate the embodiment of culture in mental life, of culturally facilitated cognitive processes. Rogoff (2003, p. 271) provided examples of cognition *beyond the skull*, noting that "cognition is distributed across individuals, other people, and cultural tools and institutions," thereby making learning a social relational *and* cultural process.

A culturally and ecologically embedded system will embrace the concepts of plasticity, emergence, adaptation through multiple pathways, risk and resilience, and the need to belong and to perform with competence. Cultural diversity is an essential feature, not a sidebar, to the study of human development (Raeff, 2016), and aggregating knowledge in the service of making generalizable

Box 3 Understanding Learning as Inherently Cultural and Racialized

Na'ilah Suad Nasir

Whereas classical theories of learning have viewed learning from a behaviorist, cognitivist, or sociocultural perspective, recent science deepens these understandings and enables learning to be seen in multifaceted and complex ways along several dimensions (Nasir et al., 2020). Learning involves all of the aspects captured in these learning theories and, in addition, learning is intertwined in the learning space with developmental processes involving emotion, identity, and being in relationship to self, peers, and adults (Immordino-Yang, 2016). Learning is also cultural in nature and racialized in ways that have been elaborated in research across disciplines, including psychology, anthropology, sociology, and the learning sciences. Such an elaborated science of learning is critical if we are to construct theories of learning that afford designing schools and instruction that support deep learning for multiple, diverse communities and create equitable learning environments essential to disrupting systemic racism and other forms of inequality.

In the *Handbook of the Cultural Foundations of Learning* (Nasir et al., 2020), authors across these disciplines elaborate research findings that, taken together, elucidate several key aspects of learning that capture the complexity and diversity of learning processes. Fundamental to this view is that learning is always cultural, not just as an additive layer; learning is an *inherently* cultural process for all learners (Nasir, 2012). To best represent what we know about human complexity and diversity, we argue that a theory that captures the fundamentally cultural nature of learning must rest on four key propositions, viewing learning as:

- Rooted in our biology and in our brains, both of which science increasingly recognizes as social and cultural;
- Integrated with other developmental processes, whereby learning involves the whole person – emotion, cognition, and identity processes working together;
- Shaped through the culturally organized activities of everyday life, both in and out of school, and across the life course;
- Experienced as embodied and coordinated through social interactions with the world and others (Nasir et al., 2020).

These RISE principles recognize that learning occurs across multiple developmental niches and timescales and is deeply contextual and social. Understanding the cultural nature of learning is critical for the design of schools and school systems that build trusting relationships, provide space for identity exploration and positive identity mirroring, engage with curricula with an eye toward identity and connection, and view family and community knowledge as core to disciplinary knowledge. Importantly, this view of learning enables teachers, educational leaders, and community-based education designers to create learning spaces that respect the diversity among learners and eschew the assimilative and hegemonic design of many schools and learning spaces. This perspective also recognizes that reconceptualizing learning, and the classrooms and curricular supports that are supposed to undergird learning, and broadening the kinds of knowledge that make up "the canon," is essential to create space for the necessary positive identity work in schools and to de-settle and interrogate the construct of "race" as political and ideological, and not biological (Lee, 2017). This approach is aligned with anti-racist teaching practices and fosters embracing multiplicity and understanding learning as integral to liberation and freedom.

claims that have ecological validity must reflect this understanding (Lee, 2010). The embeddedness of the individual in culture provides an influence across the life span and a key dimension of human evolution (Immordino-Yang & Yang, 2017; Jablonka & Lamb, 2005; Osher, Cantor, et al., 2020).

2.1.4 Holism

Context and culture provide the foundation for the principle of *holism*, which means the whole defines the parts and parts define the whole (Overton, 2015). In holism, the parts do not combine through an additive process. Instead, the combination may be better understood as a multiplicative process: When the parts combine, they produce, in combination, attributes of a novel whole that do not exist in the parts in isolation. What makes living systems unique is that they change, through mutually influential individual⟺ context relations, into new, increasingly adaptive and complex forms (see Gould & Vrba, 1982; Jablonka & Lamb, 2005). The whole, through its self-organization, has unique features that are not attributes of any part. Thus, the whole is not just quantitatively greater than the sum of its parts; it is *qualitatively different* from the sum of its parts.

A classic psychological example of holism occurs among the components of a sentence. Patterns of letters form words and then particular organizations of words form sentences. Reference to a specific letter or subset of letters or to a word or subset of words will not convey the specific meaning of the sentences. In short, as Werner and Kaplan (1963) explained, the structure and function of any specific part of a system depends on the context, field, or whole of which it is a part. Its properties and functional significance – in fact its meaning – are determined by the larger whole or context.

Certainly, the pluripotential embryo we used earlier to illustrate our dynamic systems approach has changed holistically through coactions with the context, particularly culture and relationships across its life. However, these coactions also exist at the level of the cell. It is important to consider these relations next.

2.1.5 Plasticity and Malleability

Plasticity refers to the potential for developmental change in development across life (Bateson & Gluckman, 2011). Because of mutually influential relations between individuals and their complex contexts, there are multiple pathways, or directions, that developmental change may take (Baltes et al., 2006; Lerner, 1984). Therefore, the behavior that a child manifests at a specific time in life or in one specific place (e.g., a seventh-grade Algebra 1 class) is not necessarily the behavior that the child will show across all times and places in life. Because of plasticity, development is malleable. Change will occur through individual⟺context relationships, such as those that are introduced through the design of educational innovations and environments.

Of course, plasticity is not absolute, and malleability is not infinite. Plasticity is always a relative phenomenon within the developmental system because temporal events in the life of an individual may also constrain change as well as provide for it. A system that promotes change can also function to constrain it. Nevertheless, the relative plasticity in our brains and our bodies affords an optimistic story about human development – and the development of complex skills in particular. There is always potential for thriving if environments and systems are designed to develop the skills waiting to be unleashed inside each child.

Two common examples illustrating a process by which context gets into the brain and the body is the interplay between the two hormonal systems governing our responses to stress and love, mediated through the hormones cortisol and oxytocin, respectively (Perry & Szalavitz, 2006; Schore, 2016; Siegel, 2020). These hormones carry chemical messages to the brain and body, including the structures of the limbic system, which control focus, attention, memory, and emotion. The inflammatory processes that are set off or lessened, respectively, by these hormones influence the development of these structures and can begin as early as the prenatal months and produce long-lasting impacts in a child's life and health (Slavich, 2020). Protecting pregnant mothers from high levels of stress will protect the infant from these processes. Doing so will protect the developing brain from noxious influences on the normative process of synaptic pruning during the early years. Evidence for the relative plasticity of human development disproves claims of genetic reductionism and determinism and the accounts of the fixity or irremediable nature of child development, including claims about biologically based limits in academic achievement among children of a specific race/ethnicity, social class, or gender (Lerner, 2018).

2.1.6 Interpersonal Neurobiology: Relationships

Relationships between and among children and adults represent a primary process through which biological and contextual factors influence the plasticity of the developing brain and body, and mutually reinforce each other. Relationships that are reciprocal, attuned, culturally responsive, and trustful constitute a positive developmental force between children and their physical and social contexts. Such relationships help to establish individual, child-specific (*idiographic*) developmental pathways that serve as the foundation for lifelong learning, adaptation, and the integration of social, affective, emotional, and cognitive processes. These relationships produce increasingly complex biological and adaptive learning processes and will, over time, make qualitative changes to a child's genetic makeup (Bornstein, 2019a; Bronfenbrenner & Morris, 2006; Jablonka & Lamb, 2005; Slavich, 2020; Slavich & Cole, 2013).

That relationships are important is not new knowledge (e.g., Bornstein & Leventhal, 2015; Masten, 2014a; National Scientific Council on the Developing Child, 2004). However, we must operationalize "relationship" in a way that accounts for the power of relationships to shape development in constructive ways, including at the cellular level. Li and Julian (2012) operationalized "developmental relationships" as having four characteristics: (1) enduring emotional attachment; (2) reciprocity; (3) progressive complexity of joint activity; and (4) a power balance that allows for transferability to new settings. They hypothesized that these four factors are the active ingredients in effective interventions across settings (e.g., Bornstein, 2017; Li & Julian, 2012; Siegel, 2020).

The coaction of the variables involved in developmental relationships underscores the point made earlier that self-organization of the brain means that the whole, the person, is a complex living system that builds and organizes skills through individual⇔context coactions in order to attain goals (Immordino-Yang & Yang, 2017; Immordino-Yang et al., 2019). Whether we discuss the brain, the mind, or the person, we are discussing embodied constructs that are all fundamentally relational (Overton, 2015).

2.1.7 Neural Integration

Neuroscience studies the energy flow of the brain via brain imaging studies and electroencephalograms. These methods illuminate the way that different areas of the brain consume and use energy. The degree and localization of this arousal and activation within the brain (this flow of energy) directly shapes neural circuitry and mental processes. The developing mind reflects the social, emotional, and cognitive processes by which differentiated elements of the brain become linked and integrated into a functional whole. Patterns of relationships throughout life and emotional communication are the central organizing processes for the development of the brain, and these patterns reflect the capabilities of an evolving and developing mind (Immordino-Yang & Damasio, 2007; Siegel, 2020).

As brain structures become linked and integrated, it is possible to see, literally, how the whole becomes different from the sum of the parts. In biological terms, the brain's malleability and relative plasticity produce more linkages and integration. In mathematical terms, we see the manifestations of self-organization of the brain in its increasing cohesion, coherence, and complexity, where the math of quantum mechanics, not the fixed, rigid predictive formulae of Newtonian physics, accounts for the emergence of new capabilities and skills.

In other words, multiple neural systems, not merely those historically associated with cognition, contribute to core learning processes, such as attention, concentration, memory, knowledge transfer, metacognition, motivation, and generalization. The molecular and behavioral interrelations integrated within these systems are particularly noteworthy in the case of emotion and cognition, which many cultural assumptions have dichotomized (Cantor et al., 2019; Fischer & Bidell, 2006; Immordino-Yang & Damasio, 2007; Osher, Cantor, et al., 2020). In fact, in the context of human relationships, emotion and cognition co-organize all human thought and activity and are inextricably linked.

2.1.7 Adaptive Epigenesis

Positive development and thriving (Lerner, 2004) emerge from the integration of several individual and contextual systems, from the biological and physiological to the cultural and historical (e.g., Spencer, 2006). In this dynamic, relational developmental systems framework, the life cycle of an organism is not prefigured in a genetic program (Bogard et al., 2017; Keller, 2010; Lewontin et al., 1984; Moore, 2015). Rather, genes act as chemical followers, not prime movers, in developmental processes (Hubbard & Wald, 1999; Pigliucci & Mueller, 2010; West-Eberhard, 2003).

There are approximately 20,000 genes in the human genome. As packages of biological instructions, genes require signals to determine which processes are carried out, with social and physical contexts influencing if, when, how, and which genes are expressed (Moore, 2015; Slavich & Cole, 2013). The process of transcribing DNA into RNA involves the actions of many other chemicals (proteins), often more than 100 (Harper, 2005). The activity of these other proteins defines the process of *epigenetics*. The term "epi" comes from the Greek and means "over" or "above," indicating that epigenetic effects are effects that are "beyond" the effects of genes (Misteli, 2013).

This conception of development runs counter to genetic reductionist views of evolutionary change that see genes as the primary cause of, or mover in, human development (e.g., Burt, 1966; Eysenck, 1979; Lorenz, 1940, 1966; Plomin, 2018; Rushton, 2000). Genetic reductionist ideas have been found to be both egregiously flawed, often counterfactual, and frequently racist (e.g., Gould, 1996; Ho & Saunders, 1984; Joseph, 2015; Lerner, 1992; Panofsky, 2014; Rose & Rose, 2000). Critiques of genetic reductionism indicate that dynamic systems concepts are scientifically sound and support the view that the results of contemporary, cutting-edge research in biology, epigenetics, and medicine tell an optimistic story about what is possible for the pluripotential embryo as it expresses its genetic influence through the lived experiences and relationships it is exposed to. This expression is the developmental story of human potential itself. In addition, these critiques apply to trait theories that posit that temperament, intelligence, resilience, and personality are determined by genes (Lerner, 2018) and to conceptions of development as a static, fixed-stepped ladder (Fischer & Bidell, 2006; Lerner & Overton, 2017).

Epigenetic adaptation is the biological process through which the ecology of relationships, experiences, perceptions, and physical and chemical toxins get "under the skin" and influence lifelong learning, behavior, neural integration, and health (Bernstein et al., 2007). Chemical signals derived from environmental influences – "epigenetic signatures" – affect when and how genes are switched on and off, and whether gene change is temporary or permanent. This process begins before conception (via parental experiences and cultural histories) and contributes to the transmission of behaviors and experiences to future generations (e.g., Keating, 2016; Meaney, 2010), as well as to qualitative changes in humans' genetic makeup, both within and across generations (Moore, 2015; Slavich, 2020; Slavich & Cole, 2013).

Indeed, Jablonka and Lamb (2005) presented evidence that contemporary research in molecular biology indicates clearly that neo-Darwinian assumptions about the role of genes in evolution (i.e., that genes are the unit of analyses and, as well, the driver of evolution) are mistaken. This research demonstrates that cells can transmit information to daughter cells through non-DNA, or epigenetic, means. Furthermore, Jablonka and Lamb (2005) asserted that there are psychological processes and cultural processes that add two additional dimensions to the process of evolution, beyond genetics and epigenetics. They explained that humans "inherit" symbols – particularly language and histories – from their parents, and growth and adaptiveness over their life span thus reflect the integration of the symbolic constructs of culture.

2.1.8 Emergence

The concept of *emergence* pertains to the appearance of *novelty*, of *transformation (qualitative change), in the development of a human being*. In the history of the biological and the social/behavioral sciences, a focus on emergence arose to oppose ideas of reductionism including the primacy of genes as the sole drivers of development. As dynamic systems models of development were introduced (e.g., Fischer & Bidell, 2006; Molenaar et al., 2014; von Bertalanffy, 1933) and the concepts of embodiment and holism were understood, the concept of emergence was increasingly used to describe and explain novelty in development of a human being.

Emergence is regarded as a core feature of *epigenesis* (Gottlieb, 1998). Epigenesis helps to explain the existence of transformational variation, the appearance (emergence) of nonexpected attributes, and nonlinearity of developmental change. Each of the classic grand developmental theories of the twentieth century – Bloom (1984), Erikson (1959), Piaget (1970), Vygotsky (1978), and Werner (1948) – pointed to the centrality of nonlinearity and emergence, including the emergence of new, increasingly complex and adaptive skills. All these theorists noted that developmental attributes from prior levels of development will combine to create a subsequent "new" developmental level, producing (through their dynamic combination) attributes and skills that did not exist in the prior levels.

In summary, emergence means that novel characteristics (crawling being replaced by upright posture and walking, one-word utterances into two-word sentences, "sudden insight" about the solution to a problem, or using hypotheses and formal reasoning to think about the world) will occur because human development is an open system. And newness means that something now exists that was not present before, either in smaller or even in precursory form. Epigenetic development means that there will be an emergence of characteristics, both adaptive and not, supporting survival or not, and that these skills and capabilities will be designed in response to a new period of development, and they were not present in any precursory form before their time of appearance. Emergent, epigenetic changes are an instance of inheritance not solely dependent on our genes but passed to future generations.

2.1.9 Variation, Jaggedness, and Pathways

Variation is the essence of the human condition (Darwin, 1859, 1872; Gould, 1996). All people have (1) some attributes in common with all other people (e.g., all humans have nervous systems, circulatory systems, respiratory systems, etc.) and (2) attributes that they share with only some other people (e.g., males have one type of reproductive system and females have another type of reproductive system) (Emmerich, 1968; Kluckhohn & Murray, 1948). However, no two people have exactly the same genetic composition, even identical twins (e.g., Moore, 2015). Every person has a unique history of individual⇔context relations. Therefore, as Rose (2016) explained, using an average score for a sample or population cannot ever adequately represent the full set of attributes of any person in the sample or population.

In addition, an individual's attributes – the "scores" for, say, complex math, reading, and writing skills; for personality or character attributes; for motivational characteristics; for interests, attitudes, and values – have specific and different magnitudes at any point in the individual's life. The pace, direction, and quality of development will vary for each person across life, as each person encounters a *specific sequence of experiences in specific contexts*. Each individual will have *unique pathways* across their childhood, as the sequence of individual⇔context relations that comprises their specific life course unfolds. As Rose (2016) described, each child "walks the road less traveled" because every individual will have their own specific history of development across time and place.

The implications for educators will be understanding that the acquisition of complex academic skills and knowledge is a profoundly nonlinear process (Dawson, 2020; Granott, 2020). It is, in fact, *jagged*. Such skills develop in fits and starts with forward movement and backward transitions. Backward transitions are important to understand because they are a frequent feature of novel skill development and emergence. Sometimes they have to do with further consolidation of a lower-level skill, or reflect that another dimension of an academic skill is yet to be mastered, or that influences come from the external worlds of a child at just the right time to bring new dimensions of complex skills to light (e.g., Vygotsky 1978). This variation is the nature of the development of all learning skills.

Overall, the salient point is that all development and learning is nonlinear. This nonlinearity has enormous implications for education systems, including the ways we assess performance and competency and the ways learning environments do or do not reveal the talents and skills that students possess. Jaggedness and its developmental course mean that each child has a developmental range of competency and each child has some scores above average, some scores below average, and perhaps even a few scores that fit an average (Bornstein & Putnick, 2019). But, importantly, no one score, and no average score, can adequately represent the breadth of abilities or potential of a child (the child's specific developmental range).

In past decades, educators may have been appropriately perplexed about how to deal with such person-specific complexity. In recent years, Rose (2016) and other developmental scientists (most notably Molenaar & Nesselroade, 2014, 2015) have advanced statistical methods (e.g., dynamic factor analysis, Idiographic Filtering) to describe, explain, and suggest ideas for optimizing the educational pathways and, more generally, for promoting thriving across the life span of each specific child.

2.1.10 The Constructive Web

Complex skills in a human being, including learning skills, are structures that reflect the integrating, self-organizing properties of our developing brains. They are bringing together the systems of feeling, thinking, and acting, within a particular sociocultural context, toward particular goals (for example, in a school or a classroom or a ballfield) (e.g., Hardway, 2020). The development of a complex skill reflects a child's growing ability to exert control – to manifest agency – over their sociocultural context (Li, 2020). New, complex academic skills emerge slowly across time and place, as individuals coordinate lower-level elements of acting, thinking, and feeling into higher-order complex academic skills that *transfer* into new domains of action and contexts. These processes reflect the *agency* of the child. Agency *activates* neuronal pathways and *patterns of pathways* of increasing synaptic strength. *Representations* of histories and experience are laid down in our increasingly *complex self-organized brains*. These changes are happening in the context of environments, meaningful instructional learning experiences, and hopefully rich, positive developmental relationships across the multiple settings in a child's life.

A powerful representation of dynamic, complex skill development is embodied in the concept of the "constructive web" (Fischer & Bidell, 2006). The constructive web deepens our thinking about the progressive, nonlinear, and adaptive nature of complex skill development. The concept points to an active process between the child and multiple relational agents, that is to coactions with the specific contexts in the life of a child, and thus through multiple pathways across those contexts. The resulting skills and behaviors are joint products of the child and the resources and relationships that compose their context (of the child's individual⇔context relations). The constructive web concept emphasizes the core characteristics of human development: malleability, context, jaggedness, person-specific pathways, the developmental continuum across time and place, and thus the integration of the individual and the individual's complex and changing context. The interplay between individual and context is expressed as progressive neural integration through pathways of increasingly stable synaptic strength in the developing brain through its progressive organization and reorganization as a complex system across the life span.

A complex skill produced by a web-like integrated process of development means that even the most discrete skill, for example the ability to solve an algebraic word problem, has to account for the embodied person learning that skill. Thus, developmental concepts and their sequencing encompass things like prior experience, history, culture, foundational skill development, identity, agency, and motivation. All these attributes will be present as the whole person develops. If educators teach to the discrete math skill, some children will "learn it"; but, if they teach to the embodied person, then, importantly, children will learn the discrete skill, and they will want to learn more and also discover parts of themselves – their interests, talents, and new thinking and analytic capabilities – as they learn this skill (e.g., Steenbeek & van Geert, 2020). Children whose developmental beginnings have been compromised may, under appropriate conditions (Bloom, 1984), learn these skills as well, including the ability to progress and attain higher-order knowledge, thinking, and analytic skills. The design of learning settings as well as adult preparation for producing those kinds of formal and informal learning experiences for children are different endeavors from teaching content or simple skills.

Teaching and learning experiences that are rigorous and designed for the whole child should become experiences based on the principles laid out in this section – experiences defined by the macroconditions, microprocesses, experiences, and relationships that produce them. Such teaching and learning will lead to the mutual discovery of a child's entire developmental range and the fullest expression of what a child can do as he or she learns, contributes to the community, and thrives in life. Sometimes this development happens organically, for example, when a child witnesses someone demonstrating a more advanced version of a skill being learned. However, intentional educational steps can be taken to promote children's ability to see what they are truly capable of and build their identities, interests, and passions.

2.1.11 Developmental Range

The operationalization of developmental range is the doorway to the development of all complex skills; it is the biological expression of what each child is capable of – their inner potential. Our view is that a new, twenty-first century approach to education, one based on the web-like nature of dynamic, complex skills, means that children whose developmental beginnings have been compromised in any way will also be exposed to a vision of their talents and assets, and use their agency in the service of building new adaptive complex skills including the highest-order academic and problem-solving skills. This issue – the ability to see and create opportunities for growth in developmental range – is the feature of adult preparation and environmental design that is most directly tied to the awareness and realization of the potential that exists inside each child and should be the design challenge to educators, practitioners, and researchers that arises out of the insights and conclusions presented in this Element. Developmental range is the concept in this Element that has the greatest implication for the design of all learning settings and the preparation of adults within them.

Skill development is variable and varies with context. There are no fixed patterns of intelligence or learning styles, and there are no fixed stages or fixed endpoints. A child who can solve a math problem at night with parents may not be able to solve the same problem in the classroom the next day. Skills therefore exist as a range of levels, not a specific level, depending on variables like context, emotional state, time of day, and social partners.

Developmental range is a particularly important concept for understanding learning, academic rigor, and performance. Because skills are "context-sensitive control structures" (Fischer & Bidell, 2006; Mascolo & Fischer, 2015), they reflect a person's capacity to exert control over thinking, feeling, and acting within a particular sociocultural context (home, classroom, peer group, sports, or interest club). The performance of any skill, especially a newly developing skill, can have a great range of levels of performance based on contextual factors including emotional state, safety, language, prior history, positive peer groups, and setting conditions. This broad set of context-ual factors, likely more than anything, contributes to the great variability in skill acquisition and performance seen in the classrooms, ballfields, and other child-serving settings. Moreover, the concept of developmental range means that any single measure of a child's ability – especially a standardized measure (e.g., such as a test of intelligence) (Richardson, 2017), purported to index a general degree of capacity of a child – cannot reflect the variability in performance and ability that the child can show across the range of contexts within which they occur.

A child's optimal level of performance is the level of skill, within a particular domain, that the child is capable of, using agency under conditions of coactive guided participation (e.g., effective scaffolding) by another person (Vygotsky, 1978). High support of this kind refers to adult practices that direct children's attention toward the relevant parts of a task (e.g., Bloom, 1984). A child's performance under these conditions will be higher than the child's functional level under conditions of normal support. Children will show distinct levels of competence under different levels of support, and this variation is what is meant by *developmental range* (e.g., Bloom, 1984; Vygotsky, 1978). The contextual variation associated with the manifestation of developmental range provides insight into the nuanced ways in which thriving (optimal behavior and devel-opment) (Masten, 2014b) can be instantiated through changes in indivi-dual⇔context relations.

It is helpful to distinguish between a student's scaffolded performance versus optimal performance under conditions of high support. High support can occur based on the way a classroom is structured or the way a lesson is presented. Scaffolding is different from high support because, in scaffolding, the expert is either performing part of the task or giving sufficient instruction such that the child does something the child could not have done alone. Many complex skills are learned or previewed by children with the support of scaffolding. With scaffolding, children are able to move across a phase in their development from the point of not showing the possession of a skill to the point of having the skill. These two points in development have been termed by Vygotsky (1978) as the "zone of proximal development" (ZPD). Support in the ZPD through coactions with another person, who could be a parent, sibling, or peer (Rhodes, 2020), is a crucial step toward competence and mastery for many children. Providing scaffolding (support of a learner across the ZPD) is often an important teaching skill (and parenting skill) because it enables the adult to promote a child discovering the fullest expression of their developmental range.

In the ZPD, a child learning new skills with the assistance of others, including peers and siblings, is able to "preview" or accomplish something in advance of this level of skill being fully acquired or internalized. Providing experiences such that children can preview their future capabilities is crucial for the cultivation of belief, confidence, and most importantly, an awareness by a student of their potential. Conversely, experiences of stereotype threat, race/ethnicity, and gender assumptions will contribute to the underdevelopment of skills, "underpitching" in the rigor of instructional experiences and an undermining of a student's belief in themselves as learner.

The relational/social dimensions of this kind of scaffolding are also considered in the literature describing developmental relationships (Li & Julian, 2012). Positive human relationships serve multiple psychological and developmental purposes. These purposes include attachment, trust, and stress reduction, and sharing control in the development of the complex skill itself.

Another example of developmental relationships is ecological scaffolding, when aspects of the social context are designed to support higher performance. For example, an environment may be designed to be safe, so that children feel they can take risks in their own growth and performance. Such relationships may lead to self-scaffolding, which occurs when a person who has learned a problem-solving technique transfers and applies the technique to a new situation.

2.2 Learning to Read

In the standard metaphor for development, children are assessed along a single, unidirectional developmental ladder with an underlying assumption among educators that students move along this one ladder toward competency and mastery in a specific skill. The constructive web framework provides tools for rethinking the variability in skill development and individual developmental range. When children are seen as moving along different pathways, a teacher's work is changed from forcing students to learn in one way to finding the best pathways for children to follow to express their developmental range. Different children learn different skills along different pathways toward a final endpoint – competency and mastery in a given skill, thus reflecting the concept of *equifinality*, of a common final endpoint in development (Lerner, 2018).

The acquisition of reading skills serves as one example of dynamic, context-embedded skill construction across different pathways. Reading skills are embedded in, and influenced by, children's exposures to literacy and the cultures in which children are situated. As with other skills, there is significant variability, multiple cultural influences, and variable synaptic strength in the pathways by which children develop literacy. Although the nature of literacy has since expanded (e.g., to internet-related literacies), Knight and Fischer's (1992) identification of multiple pathways to literacy remains useful when we think about the development of particular literacies. When children's performance is assessed relative to the most common pathway, it can only be viewed as either "normal" or "delayed," with remediation directed toward speeding up progress along the "normal" pathway. Yet, we now know that slower readers can be viewed as following *different* pathways to become skilled readers, rather than as "delayed" based on a presumed universal pathway. In this way, the constructive web supports reconceptualizing developmental and cultural differences as alternative pathways rather than as deficits.

Simultaneously, the concept of the constructive web highlights the opportunity for instructional and curricular designs that enhance access to these alternative pathways, and in so doing, channel student effort toward the pathway where individual progress and motivation to learn will be greatest. Such steps will serve to optimize developmental range and literacy development for all students (Fischer et al., 2007; Knight & Fischer, 1992).

The example of learning to read highlights principles that can generalize to other domain-specific learning activities and outcomes – most notably, the profound role of developmental variability, including unique pathways, pacing, and range, and the need to situate and integrate fundamental neural processes in contexts that promote developmental progression and the expression of developmental range. Figure 1 illustrates a constructive web for reading, learning, and performance from data reported by Mascolo and Fischer (2015).

The acquisition of academic and learning skills and the learning sciences are but one example of the developmental concepts presented in this Element. The range of students' skills – and, ultimately, their potential as human beings – can be significantly influenced through the intentional design of learning environments and experiences to optimize their development under conditions of high, personalized support (Fischer & Bidell, 2006).

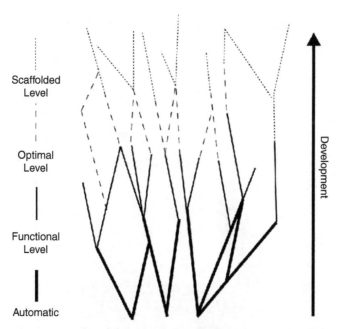

Figure 1 The constructive developmental web (from Fischer & Bidell, 2006). An individual functions at multiple levels at any time in life; the web reflects the multidirectional nature of development across time and place.

An example of a developmental framework intended to support innovations for applying the principle of the constructive web is the Building Blocks for Learning (BBFL) framework (Stafford-Brizard, 2016). This framework is derived from research within diverse literatures and converges on the knowledge that multiple neural systems, and not only cognitive attributes, contribute to the core and essential processes involved in learning (Stafford-Brizard, 2016). Brooke Stafford-Brizard provides deeper commentary on the BBFL in Box 4.

BBFL was specifically designed as a developmental and learning framework that assumes different developmental starting points, where contextual factors, such as the experience of trauma, can interrupt the development of foundational skills. Stafford-Brizard recognized its power as a wellness framework because of the embedded pathways for adaptive skills, such as social awareness, belonging, resilience, curiosity, and civic engagement. As illustrated in Figure 2, this framework demonstrates the progressive nature of skill development, where foundational skills lay the groundwork for higher-order skills, all of which underpin the acquisition of domain-specific skills and their ultimate mastery. Collectively, the integration of affective, cognitive, social, and emotional processes merging into habits, skills, and mindsets yields many different types of

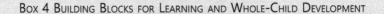

Box 4 Building Blocks for Learning and Whole-Child Development

Brooke Stafford-Brizard

Mounting evidence demonstrates that development of the individual cannot be disentangled from the context in which that individual develops, including political and sociocultural elements of context. Such evidence reinforces that these elements must become central when leveraging developmental frameworks like the BBFL (Stafford-Brizard, 2016), which theorizes the role that cognitive and affective skills and mindsets play in supporting whole-child development. *Developmental frameworks might be universal, including constructs relevant to all human beings, but they cannot be color blind.* Therefore, when accessing such a framework to inform the design and delivery of equitable learning environments and experiences for children, researchers and educators must prioritize the role that a sociocultural element such as racial identity plays in development (Nasir et al., 2020). *This focus cannot be an additional or supplementary one; this focus is integral to how constructs within the framework are operationalized and how they develop and coact with each other within the framework as a whole.*

Self-regulation is an example. Within the BBFL, self-regulation involves regulating attention, emotion, and executive functioning in the service of goal-directed actions (Blair & Ursache, 2011). However, without centering race and culture as critical contextual factors, this construct can easily be operationalized through a dominant or individual-istic lens, which denies the centrality of community and collective success that many cultures within our society, like those within indigenous com-munities, place on development. Rowan-Kenyon and colleagues (2018) proposed that acknowledging the interconnected role that culture, com-munity, and multifaceted development, including spirituality, play in the development of something like self-regulation is important when taking a context-sensitive and inclusive approach to whole-child development.

Beyond the role that racial identity must play in defining these con-structs, the science demonstrating the role that race and ethnicity play in an individual's experience within US society and the impact that racial-ethnic identity has on the development of BBFL skills and mindsets must become a normative presence in application. Racial-ethnic identity reinforces positive development of individual skills and mindsets within the BBFL including stress management, self-efficacy, relationships skills, and resilience (e.g., Anderson et al., 2018; Rivas-Drake et al., 2014; Umana-Taylor et al., 2018). When addressing the role that broader context plays in individual development, we cannot ignore the role that racism plays within society as a macro-stressor and source of stress for Black families (Murry et al., 2018). Racism as a macro-stressor and contributor to adversity is an important addition to other named adverse childhood experiences like neglect, abuse, and instability (Felitti et al., 1998) that impact development of BBFL skills and mindsets.

A dramatic shift in the US education system grounded in the develop-mental and learning sciences is long overdue. If we know that to learn and thrive students must bring their whole selves to the classroom then we cannot ask them to leave any part of themselves, their culture, or their community behind. This focus includes intentionally integrating strengths and assets connected to racial-ethnic identity into whole-child learning and development.

metacognitive and academic competencies that are critical to students' school and life success (Immordino-Yang & Damasio, 2007; Stafford-Brizard, 2016).

The integration of these skills with increasingly complex, relevant, and rigorous instructional experiences will produce states of domain-specific mas-tery and higher-order thinking skills. Webs and growth curves depicting know-ledge and skill development could yield more sophisticated frameworks that take into account periods of greater and lesser sensitivity, acknowledge

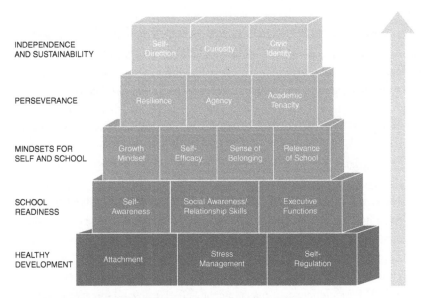

Figure 2 The BBFL framework (Stafford-Brizard, 2016).

developmental range, and involve an ability to capture convergences, plateaus, and bursts in complex skill development (Fischer & Bidell, 2006; Mascolo & Bidell, 2020; Mascolo & Fischer, 2015).

2.3 From Theory to Measurement

The developmental opportunities for thriving that become possible using the dynamic systems concepts presented in this Element may, when translated into new designs for learning settings both in and out of school, innovations in practice, and policies to bring them to scale, yield powerful evidence about capabilities in children that might not otherwise have been possible or noticed by the student or the adults around them. The opportunity to move an increasing number of children onto positive developmental learning trajectories and the fullest expression of the breadth of their developmental range will produce nuanced changes that reflect the variation and jaggedness of developmental pathways that we have described.

This conception of development offers researchers, educators, and practitioners in diverse settings the challenge and the opportunity to build an approach to measurement that can reflect the dynamic changes involved in whole-child development, learning, and thriving across settings and across ontogenetic and historical time (Elder et al., 2015). Such an approach to measurement will provide a "language" for measurement that aligns with the ideas of dynamic systems and will describe developmental change and skill development occurring for children on their individual pathways toward thriving. Even more important, this "language" for measurement will connect the contours of such pathways to specific individual⟺context relations that influence developmental change.

However, constructing measures that are sensitive to developmental change across the life span is not an easy task. Nevertheless, such measures are the basis of tools enabling the description, explanation, and optimization of opportunities for whole-child development, learning, and thriving of specific children developing in specific contexts. In Section 3, we introduce a language for measurement that describes whole-child development and the opportunities afforded by learning settings designed for thriving.

3 A *Developmental* Approach to Measuring Whole-Child Development

But what if, all along, these well-meaning efforts at closing the achievement gap have been opening the door to racist ideas? What if different environments lead to different kinds of achievement rather than different levels of achievement? What if the intellect of a low-testing black child in a poor black school is different from – and not inferior to – the intellect of a high-testing white child in a rich white school? What if we measured intelligence by how knowledgeable individuals are about their own environments? What if we measured intellect by an individual's desire to know? What if we realized the best way to ensure an effective educational system is not by standardizing our curricula and tests but by standardizing the opportunities available to all students?

Ibram X. Kendi (2019), *How to Be an Anti-Racist*

The language for measurement that has been used by developmental and educational scientists does not currently reflect what is actually happening in the development of each specific child, and it does not express what is happening in the context that is bringing about such child-specific change. The language also does not portray child⟺context relations that result in whole-child development and, in ideal circumstances, thriving. As we explain in this section, the language that is currently used focuses on purported "average" children. It emphasizes relations among variables (e.g., scores on intelligence or ability tests, personality or temperament attributes, or social-emotional skills) that are identified by studying *groups* of children, with the underlying assumption that the group score represents the scores of the individuals inside the group (Rose, 2016). Although there could be value in knowing how a specific child may be compared to such averages and/or group data, this information does not describe or communicate what has actually changed and developed in the individual child nor why.

Contrast the following communication from an educator to a parent:

> "Your child is better than average in regard to subject matter 'x,' is average on
> subject matter 'y,' but is below average on subject matter 'z'."

with a different communication from educator to parent:

> "We noticed that your child performed at Level '1' when the learning setting
> had contextual support 'x' as compared to performance at Level '2' when the
> contextual support conditions were 'y'."

The language used for assessment of specific children has not prioritized how variables coalesce to create developmental "synergies" within a specific child, developing within and across the specific places within which the child lives, at specific, successive times in life. For example, there have been few statements to parents that report something like:

> In kindergarten, the relation of contextual variables x, y, and z for your child
> showed Performance Level '1'; when your child was in the middle elemen-
> tary school grades, the relation among these contextual variables resulted in
> Performance Level '2,' and particularly so when the child was involved in an
> additional context (an out-of-school-time program): The relation was then
> Performance Level '3.'

Notice that this last statement links changes within the child to changes in the specific contextual experiences and activities with which the child was engaged. A reason that the latter statements about children are relatively rare is that intensive, child-specific measurement of children or of their specific contexts/ experiences also rarely occur. Because of the absence of such measurement, linking specific children to the specific coactive context is obviated. Because changes within the person are not ordinarily linked to each other or to changes in the context, any statements about individual⇔context relations that may be associated with thriving or the lack thereof cannot be made either.

Even when children are studied repeatedly across their lives, their attributes at one time are not typically compared to their attributes at subsequent times; that is, what are termed *ipsative* comparisons are not made (Lerner, 2018). One reason for the absence of quantitative, ipsative analyses is that person-specific (*idio-graphic*) approaches to data analysis have not been a major interest among developmental methodologists, primarily because of a focus on averages and other group or population-based statistical methods (Bornstein et al., 2017; Molenaar, 2007; Rose, 2016). A focus on averages is often rationalized by asserting that such statistics represent the true representation of a behavioral or developmental phenomenon; as such, variation around the mean is interpreted as error and, as such, not meaningful (Rose, 2016). However, the assumption that the average appropriately reflects meaningful attributes of each of the individuals whose specific scores contribute to the average is not, in fact, empirically true.

Because information about specific, within-the-person consistencies and changes are rarely gathered, or are not analyzed even if they are available, the statements that are made about average trends for a group of children have the apparent utility of adequately describing each child in the group. However, such statements are more apparent than true.

As explained by Gordon Allport (1968, p. 68):

> Whatever individuality is, it is not the residual ragbag left over after general dimensions have been exhausted.

And to paraphrase Allport: Variables are variables, averages are averages, "and people are people" (Allport, 1937, p. 400).

If scientists, educators, or parents wish to understand the dynamic and specific individual⇔context relations that we discussed in Section 2 – relations that change the embryo into a whole, thriving child – they need to be able to use language about measurement that describes the specific coactions between a child and the context that can account for the pathways from embryo to whole-child development, learning, and thriving. This section introduces such a language in the service of describing changes within a specific person happening in the specific and different settings for learning and development across the life span.

It is ironic that, at this writing at the beginning of the third decade of the twenty-first century, we need to emphasize the need for such statements in the study of development and thriving. For more than eighty years, developmental and personality scientists have agreed that the study of human development involves the study of changes within the individual (e.g., Allport, 1937, 1968; Lerner, 2012). This fundamental and obvious point is not controversial. As discussed by Bornstein (2017, 2019b), in explaining his Specificity Principle (which we discuss in greater detail later in this section), all researchers who study development would agree that what they – and parents, teachers, and other child-serving professionals – want to understand are several specific things about an individual, including:

(1) How best to *describe* specific changes within a person;
(2) How best to *explain* what specific changes occur at specific times in life for specific children living in specific contexts; and
(3) How best to *optimize* each individual's developmental change so that the probability of health and positive learning development will characterize the person's specific pathway across life.

Given the unanimity about the definition of development and the goals of studying development, it might also seem obvious that researchers studying development should use or seek to create measures that are able to detect within-the-person changes. However, across the history of the study of human development, such measurement has seldom been undertaken (Lerner, 2018). In fact, most measures used to study development have not been measures of within-person change (Rose, 2016).

It may be surprising to people not schooled in the history of measurement in the study of human development to learn that researchers in this field have studied changes in *variables* (e.g., achievement test scores, IQ scores, grit, or self-esteem) and not in *people*. For instance, as shown in Figure 2 (see Section 2), researchers using the BBFL framework (Stafford-Brizard, 2016) have studied changes in such variables as self-regulation, executive functions, growth mindset, resilience, or civic identity across the kindergarten through Grade 12 span. Researchers in the field of human development have amassed a great deal of knowledge about how to measure such variables with reliability and validity, and these researchers know if scores for variables stay the same or change across different points in the life span. Unfortunately, however, this information is *irrelevant* to describing, explaining, or optimizing any specific person's development.

Why?

3.1 The Three Essential Parts of All Measures

Whenever researchers set out to measure any facet of human development, they combine (1) a measure of a specific variable (e.g., such as self-regulation or growth mindset) for (2) a specific individual (e.g., a Latina living in New York City, El Paso, Texas, or Los Angeles, California) and at (3) a specific time of measurement (e.g., when the girl is in the third grade and, two years after the end of the COVID-19 pandemic). Said another way, whenever something is measured, the measurement involves a "score" for a specific variable, for a specific individual, and for a specific time of measurement.

An example may be useful for explaining how these three parts of all measures have been typically involved in developmental research. Imagine that a researcher is interested in the development of both self-regulation and growth mindset in elementary school students across Grades 3, 4, and 5. The researcher might enroll a sample of 100 third graders (50 boys and 50 girls) and administer measures of both self-regulation and growth mindset at the beginning of the first school year. Each student in the sample would, then, have a score for each of the two variables at this one time of measurement. Because researchers are interested in development, they might then return to the school to measure the two variables again in the same students at the beginning of the fourth grade and then at the beginning of the fifth grade. After all this data collection, the data set possessed by the researcher would have each student, measured on each of the two variables, at each of the three times of testing.

Development involves changes within an individual, and this data set could be investigated by assessing the pattern of change for *each* of the 100 children for each of the 2 variables across the 3 testing times. Starting with these assessments of each child, the researchers could then determine if they could aggregate individuals: Are there groups of individuals who change in the same or in very similar ways? In other words, starting with the study of within-person change – starting with the study of development for each person in the sample – the researchers could then see if more general statements about development were possible to make.

However, for the *vast majority* of studies undertaken in the study of human development, this within-individual analysis approach (assessing individual development first and then determining if aggregation to groups is possible) is never undertaken. The vast majority of studies proceed by first aggregating data across individuals. As noted by Rose et al. (2013):

> By analyzing statistical averages, not individuals, these models provide descriptions about global regularities in everything from cancer ... to cognition . . .. However, we argue that the value of such models ultimately depends on whether they apply to individuals; after all, a science of the group is a poor substitute for a true science of the individual. Traditional models often assume that insights about the population automatically apply to all individuals (Molenaar, 2013). This assumption is simple, it is understandable, and it is necessary to justify the use of averages to understand individuals. However, it is also wrong! (p. 152)

Returning to our example, researchers taking this "aggregate first approach" would describe the average score for self-regulation and the average score for growth mindset at the first time of measurement. To compute these averages, researchers would sum the scores for each variable and divide by 100 to determine the mean score. The researchers might also assess the way that the scores for self-regulation were related to the scores for growth mindset at the first time of testing. They would most likely compute a coefficient of correlation to express this relation. As well, the researchers would compute averages and correlations in the same way for the data that existed at the second and the third times of testing. The researchers might then assess (e.g., through statistics such as repeated-measures analyses of variance) whether the means for each variable changed across the three times of measurement. Moreover, they would compute whether the correlations between self-regulation and growth mindset varied across the three times of testing.

To conduct all these analyses, the researchers would have to have assessed how variables go together across individuals, both within each time of measurement and, because the researchers are interested in studying development, across times of measurement. However, what they have learned is how a variable – *and not any person* – may change (or not), either in mean level or in its relations with another variable. Even if the same 100 people were present at each of the 3 times of testing (if there was no drop out from the sample across the 3 grades), individuals were used only to contribute to the computation of group averages and correlations. The researcher may have learned about changes in variables, but they have learned nothing about how variables change *within* a person across his or her life.

Moreover, given our focus on dynamic, relational developmental systems models of development, the absence of measurement of context in this example would mean that any changes in variable averages or intercorrelations across time would, in effect, remain incomplete. That is, *if* there is an absence of: (1) measures of the context that may moderate the changes in variables; and (2) measures of individual⇔context relations, *then* it would not be possible to study the coactions that might have been involved in changes in either variable or their interrelations.

In addition, as in Section 2, researchers would not understand anything about a specific child's developmental range or what explains why a child's performance was at a specific part of their developmental range. A single, standardized test score cannot illuminate the ways in which a child may manifest skills across contexts, because neither repeated measures of the child, nor repeated measures of the context, have been assessed. As also noted in Section 2 and by Rose et al. (2013), understanding human development involves the study of multiple person-in-context relations. Using average scores for a group obscures both developmental range *and* the unique contextual influences, good or bad, that may exist for children in the sample – a key point we discuss again later in Section 3.8.

Indeed, as explained by Rose (2016), researchers do not know if or how the information they obtained about variables applies to any of the 100 individuals in the sample. In other words, aggregation across individuals through focusing on group statistics, such as the averages or correlations among variables involved in the example we have presented, runs the risk of failing to measure, or, at the least, misrepresenting the measurement of, developmental change. However, these problems with variable-centered analyses are not simply hypothetical issues. An example drawn from actual data illustrates this problem.

3.2 The Ram et al. (2005) Study of Emotion Change

Ram and his colleagues (2005) sought to understand if aggregated data about changes in emotions – that is, the changing presence of pleasant and unpleasant emotions in the daily lives of research participants (college students, in their example) – could be accurately represented by aggregated data. They asked what sort of developmental pattern, or model of developmental change, might represent the ups and downs of pleasant and unpleasant emotions that students might experience across some period of time (e.g., a semester). They conjectured that a reasonable model to represent such emotion changes might be a simple sinusoidal (sine) wave function – a smoothly rising and falling curve reflecting the possible ups and downs of emotions students may experience (for example, before and after a big test, before a break in classes, or after the break ends and classes begin again).

Ram and his colleagues assessed emotional states with measures that were reliable and valid to use among college students to index potential daily changes in what they termed pleasant affect (PA) and unpleasant affect (UA). Said another way, they were able to assess, among the 179 participants in their study, PA and UA on a daily basis because they had used *change-sensitive measures*. Change-sensitive measures are measures that are capable of detecting changes in an individual's functioning if, in fact, such changes exist. This feature of their study is a very important one.

Using the change-sensitive measures of PA and UA, each of the 179 college students the researchers studied responded to the measures each day for 7 weeks (49 consecutive days). When data collection was complete, Ram and his colleagues tested one type of aggregation to determine if changes in PA and UA followed a sine wave format. As we suggested, the lives of college students might be expected to vary on a weekly basis as, for instance, one week might be filled with tests (e.g., midterm exams), another week might have important assignments due, another week might be free of any deadlines, and still another week might involve spring break.

Therefore, the researchers tested a model of change that involved aggregating the data daily. Figure 3 presents the findings of tests of this model of aggregation for both PA and UA.

Figure 3 indicates that the aggregate data for the 179 students did change in a manner reflective of a sinusoidal pattern. However, although both PA and UA scores could vary from 0.0 to 8.0, variation remained close to the zero point for both measures. Positive emotions for the "average" student varied between 0.0 and +0.50, and thus variation was not seen for 7.5 points on the 8-point scale. In turn, negative emotions varied 0.0 and –0.25, and thus variation was not seen for

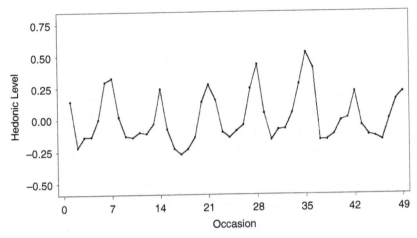

Figure 3 Daily mood – averaged across all individuals (no assessment of, or possible conclusions about, changes in any individual's mood) (from Ram et al. 2005).

7.75 points on the scale. Based on these aggregate data, it would be possible to conclude that college students, over the course of several weeks of the academic year, remained relatively neutral in their positive and negative emotions; scores hovered very close to the zero point for both emotions. To the extent there were sine wave-like variations in UA and PA, the ups and downs were fairly shallow.

If these aggregated data were truly reflective of these college students, then it would be possible to conclude that these individuals were largely stoical as tests, papers, or spring breaks occurred. Their emotional life remained basically flat as these diverse events swirled around them. If such an interpretation were valid, then – at least as the present set of authors is concerned – such stoicism does not reflect the experiences of any group of college students we have known.

However, it turned out that when the researchers inspected the day-by-day variation in PA and UA without any aggregation, they observed that the average data did not accurately represent the variation in effect for the sample of students. As shown in Figure 4, substantial variation between students in the course of within-individual change in positive and negative affect was seen. Moreover, the variation for both PA and UA ranged from +4.0 to –4.0, respectively. Clearly, there is no one aggregate pathway of change that characterized the changes seen in Figure 4. As Rose (2016) explained, all individuals walk the "road less traveled," and aggregation that ignores the individual pathways followed by each student in a sample will almost inevitably distort knowledge of development and the development of all human skills and competencies.

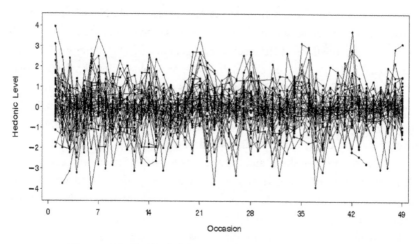

Figure 4 Individual daily mood (from Ram et al., 2005).

3.3 Why the Study of Human Development Must Include a Language for Measuring Within-Person Change and Context

The development of an individual child is not only a general phenomenon. From a whole-child perspective, informed by the ideas associated with dynamic developmental systems models, individual development is also person-specific, or *idiographic* (Molenaar & Nesselroade, 2015; Rose, 2016). In fact, when such within-person analyses have been conducted, the evidence indicates that pathways across the studied portions of life differ across individuals. Indeed, no two individuals – including monozygotic twins (Joseph, 2015; Molenaar, 2014; Richardson, 2017) – share identical developmental trajectories. No two people follow the same time-ordered set of individual⇔context relations across life (Lerner, 2018).

Consistent with the finding in life-course sociology that there is always more within-group variance than between-group variance (Elder, 1998; Elder et al., 2015), Kluckhohn and Murray (1948) also noted that each person is like no other person. That is, they pointed out that each person possesses specific, individually distinct attributes, and as a result, follows individually distinct pathways across life (Bornstein, 2017, 2019b; Rose, 2016).

3.4 Idiography: A Person-Specific Approach to the Study of Development

The process of individual development involves specific individual⇔context relations across time and place (Elder et al., 2015). As a consequence, human development is fundamentally *idiographic* (Molenaar & Nesselroade, 2015; Rose, 2016). Therefore, within dynamic systems models focused on an individual's specific relations with specific components of the ecology of human development (e.g., Mascolo & Bidell, 2020; Mascolo & Fischer, 2015; Rose, 2016), the individuality of all humans – that is, the diversity of human development in regard to every child in the world – is a primary fact of development. No one would question that the embryo described in Section 2 of this Element will evolve into a human being distinct from other human beings because of the environments, relationships, and experiences to which the embryo is exposed. This conception of the diversity of individual experience and growth has important implications for developmental methodology and for the questions asked in developmental research.

Based on the *ergodic theorems*, the standard approach to statistical analysis in the social and behavioral sciences is derived from mathematical assumptions regarding the constancy of phenomena across people and, critically, time (Molenaar, 2013). If the concept of ergodicity is applied to the study of human development, then within-person variation across time would either be ignored or treated as error. However, both the theoretical ideas discussed in Section 2 and data such as those reported by Ram et al. (2005) converge in indicating that there is meaningful variation in development across people, across contexts, and across time. These facts of human development are not consistent with the ergodic theorems. Simply, *human developmental processes are nonergodic.*

Molenaar and Nesselroade (2015) developed statistical procedures (methods such as Idiographic Filtering and Dynamic Factor Analysis) to capture the nonergodic nature of a person's changes, and at the same time, determine if generalizations beyond specific individuals are empirically warranted. As such, differences between people in their specific developmental trajectories and aggregation among individuals, when justified by the findings of longitudinal research, can be identified by the research methods used by Molenaar and Nesselroade (and others, e.g., Ram & Grimm, 2015; von Eye et al., 2015).

Therefore, both person-specific and group information may be obtained in the approach to measurement we are recommending, and, as such, neither educators nor policymakers need to choose between using information about an individual versus information about a group. Both may be used integratively (Molenaar & Nesselroade, 2015). The Bornstein Specificity Principle contributes to the language needed in developmental science to discuss person and contextual specificity and to enable data to be collected about what is idiographic and what is general in the course of human development (see Allport, 1937, 1968).

3.5 The Specificity Principle

The Specificity Principle (Bornstein, 2017, 2019b) involves researchers asking multipart questions when conducting programmatic research exploring the function, structure, and content of development of diverse groups of individuals across the life span. For instance, in seeking to understand how diverse groups of individuals may have a specific series of individual⇔context relations associated with adaptive, healthy, or positive development, researchers might undertake programs of research framed by a multipart question such as:

- What specific features of thriving are emerging;
- How they are linked to a specific trajectory of individual⇔context relations;
- For a child possessing what specific set of individual psychological, behavioral, and demographic characteristics;
- Living in what specific family, school, faith community, neighborhood, nation, culture, and physical ecology;
- At what specific points in ontogenetic development (i.e., periods of life); and
- At what specific historical period, for example, before, during, or after a major, nonnormative historical event (such as the Great Depression of the 1930s, World War II, 1939–45, or the 2020–1 COVID-19 pandemic)?

To illustrate the use of the specificity principle in a research agenda comparable to the one envisioned in our approach to whole-child development, learning, and thriving, consider the statement by Shonkoff (2017). In the paper, *"Building a System for Science-Based R&D That Achieves Breakthrough Outcomes at Scale for Young Children Facing Adversity,"* Shonkoff (2017) asks how his approach to early childhood research and development is different from current best practices. Reflecting the nonergodic and idiographic approach involved in the specificity principle, he wrote:

> The conventional definition of an "evidence-based" program is met by a statistically significant difference on average between a measured outcome in a group that received an intervention (which typically includes multiple components that are not defined precisely) and that same outcome assessed in a control or comparison group. We believe that assessing program effects on average misses what may work exceptionally well for some and poorly (or not at all) for others. Moreover, attempting to create a single "did it work?" test for a multi-faceted intervention obscures its active ingredients, leaving only a "black box" that must be adopted in its entirety. (p. 4)

Shonkoff (2017) pursued a research agenda that poses a set of questions that reflect the necessary disaggregation and specification described by Bornstein (2017). That is:

- *What about the program works*? If researchers and practitioners understand the active ingredients, they are better able to replicate and scale them.
- *How does it work*? Being specific about the processes of individual⇔context relations can help researchers and practitioners increase the impact of the program and help assure that program benefits will be sustained when the program is transported to other contexts.
- *For whom does it work and for whom does it not work*? When researchers and practitioners know more about who is and is not responding, they can scale what works for the former and make changes for the latter.
- *Where [and when] does it work*? If researchers and practitioners specify and understand the relevant contextual factors, then they are better able to make adaptations so that the program will also work in a multitude of diverse settings.

Therefore, one key outcome of such specificity principle-framed research can be the identification of the diverse ways in which individual⇔context relations may capitalize on the potential for plasticity in human life and promote thriving (Spencer et al., 2015). In essence, then, such research may illuminate specific individual⇔context relations linked to both positive and negative trajectories for specific individuals or groups of individuals. Developmental scientists and eventually practitioners of all kinds could use this information to promote those contextual factors and conditions that are most likely to support thriving for many more children.

3.6 Toward a New Approach to Measuring Learning and Development in Context

Rather than begin the analysis of developmental data with average scores and ignore the jaggedness of individuals around those scores, the Specificity Principle of Bornstein and the person-specific methods created by Molenaar, Nesselroade, and colleagues begin with the jagged, unique, and idiographic features of a specific child. Next, they begin to look for patterns across other specific children, and then, finally, determine the extent to which an average that accurately accounts for jaggedness and child-specific pathways can be modeled and utilized. These pathways involve the child's relations to specific contexts experienced across time. As such, there is analogous work occurring to develop change-sensitive and setting-specific measures of the context (e.g., Bornstein & Leventhal, 2015; Theokas & Lerner, 2006).

Understanding the patterns of jaggedness that exist in the diverse settings within which a child learns and develops (the family, classrooms, youth development or sports programs, libraries or music programs), and relations of these patterns to the features of a specific setting, will reveal core features of learning environments that are equipped to respond to *jagged* learning pathways for skill development. This focus, we believe, will promote academic growth for many more students, revealing the skills and talents that many students have. As we have emphasized, this focus must attend to the individual child, to the context of the child, and to the mutually influential relations – the dynamics – of the child⟺context relation.

3.7 Of Bob Dylan and Fish in Lakes

In his 1964 song, "Ballad in Plan D" (from the album *Another Side of Bob Dylan*), Dylan wondered, "Are birds free from the chains of the skyway?" His question conveys the idea that the flight of a bird is not independent of the context – the skyway – within which it occurs. His lyric reflects the *relational* view of the world inherent in both quantum mechanics and dynamic, developmental systems theories. The specific attributes of a bird's flight (e.g., its direction, elevation, and velocity) occur in relation to the specific atmospheric conditions of the skyway (e.g., the barometric pressure, temperature, and wind conditions) within which the flight occurs. Change the context of the bird, change the skyway, and the flight will vary.

Consider too the fish in a lake. Is the quality of a specific fish caught in a lake – its age, length, and weight – merely an outcome of its unfolding development? Alternatively, are these attributes of the fish merely products of the qualities of the lake (e.g., its water temperature, depth, and amount of bottom vegetation)? If so, then all other fish of the variety of the caught fish (say a small-mouthed bass) should possess, at the same age (i.e., length of time living in the lake), corresponding lengths and weights. However, most people experienced in fishing in the lake would attest to the fact that no two small-mouthed bass – even if the lake was stocked with fish of the same age and genetics (e.g., clones) – would come out exactly the same. Something in the *relation* between the fish and the lake creates this variation, something that may involve the fact that the lake is likely not uniform and has microenvironments that drive resilience, adaptation, and variation. Timing also matters.

Of course, the fish is not to be blamed for being too small. Nor can you blame the lake. The explanation of the variation in size lies in the specifics of a particular fish–lake relation, just as the explanation of the flight of a specific bird lies in the specifics of the bird–sky chain relation.

To this point, measurement systems of researchers and educators have been largely focused on measurement of the "fish," using average-based measurement to do so. They have not measured context in such a way as to better understand the "fish," and they have not been measuring the relation between the two to better understand the effects of context (the lake) on the fish, or the fish on the context (the lake). So, from the perspective of measurement, we have assumed fish to be similar and the lake to be uniform, neither of which is true.

In summary, attributes of the fish and of the lake are not only related; they are mutually influential: fish⇔lake! This coaction exists of course between a child and the context: child⇔context. We believe that, if this relation could be better understood and measured, the educational path of each child and each context could be enhanced. We discuss next a project aimed at furthering just such understanding and measurement.

3.8 Measurement Practices: The Measures and Methods Across the Development Continuum (MMDC) Project

If the goal of education is to understand and optimize each child's development (as we believe it should be), then our current methods and measurement approaches too often fall short. Extant methods often take an "aggregate first approach," assembling an average score of measures for an individual student as if the average were a proxy for the developing skills inside the student. Studying measurement this way gives information about how a variable (e.g., growth mindset) differs across individuals and time (for example, before and after an intervention, or at the beginning and end of a school year). The "aggregate first approach" reveals information primarily about how variables change, not about the pattern of how any individual student acquired or did not acquire that skill.

However, the Science of Learning and Development (SoLD) Alliance undertook a contrasting approach to developmental and educational measurement in the MMDC project. The project was designed to explore child-specific (idiographic) developmental trajectories across thirty to fifty measurement occasions spanning about three months of the academic year for students across the kindergarten to Grade 12 span (e.g., Yu et al., 2020). The BBFL framework presented in Figure 2 was used to study the specific pathways diverse groups of children must traverse, no matter their starting point in life, to attain the developmental and learning attributes needed for success in school and in life (Stafford-Brizard, 2016).

The BBFL framework depicts the pathways for learning, cognitive development, and academic and life success across five levels or tiers of interconnected skill development. Learning and cognitive development rest on the possession of foundational skills, including positive social attachments, stress management, executive function, and self-regulation, each conceived of as a set of skills that all children would have the opportunity to develop in an equitable world (a world in which access to opportunity and robust equity define the prevalent conditions). In that context, the possession of these attributes would enable children to develop skills that prepare them for success when entering school. These crucial skills form the foundation for the development of higher-order skills such as self-direction, curiosity, resilience, perseverance, and civic identity.

Adversity itself can be a springboard to the development of these very skills, but the existence of significant hardship and barriers to opportunity can prevent children from experiencing thriving. The BBFL framework is, then, simultaneously, a learning framework, a wellness framework, and a prevention framework against the effects of trauma (Cantor, 2020). If educational contexts were intentionally designed to develop the skills included in this framework, especially if intentionality is coupled with dismantling the barriers derived from institutional racism and white supremacy, many of the challenges that arise from exposure to adversity would be surmounted by the capacities to adapt, grow, learn, and even thrive in the course of life events, even challenging ones (Stafford-Brizard, 2016). And if such conditions and this kind of holistic, integrated development were built into *all* the varied settings in which children grow and learn, the opportunities for thriving would be significantly expanded (Cantor, 2020). The BBFL framework provides the contexts of child learning and development with an empirical roadmap for building these skills for children, no matter where they start their developmental journey, even if it includes experiences of trauma (Cantor, 2020; Stafford-Brizard, 2016).

At this writing, the MMDC project is still in an initial phase of research. MMDC researchers are measuring three of the constructs within the BBFL framework – *Intentional Self-Regulation (ISR), Executive Function (EF), and Relationship Skills (RS)* – among children in Grades 3 to 12 (Yu et al., 2020). These constructs represent key skill sets needed for thriving pathways to be established and enacted across the subsequent tiers of the BBFL framework. Prior, variable-centered research has shown that ISR, EF, and RS are positively interrelated and linked to other variables such as resilience and growth mindset (e.g., Dweck, 2016; Masten, 2014a; McClelland et al., 2015). The presence of these interrelations suggests that, if we study these constructs in an integrated manner, we can deepen understanding of how combinations of these foundational skills promote tipping points toward the development of higher-order skills (Stafford-Brizard, 2016). However, these constructs have not been studied through an approach that focused on child-specific, interrelated change.

Therefore, the goals of this initial work were to determine (1) Do meaningful *individual* pathways of development of these three constructs exist? and (2) Are these pathways adequately represented by averages across participants? The answers to these questions are "yes" and "no," respectively. To illustrate, we first summarize findings about longitudinal changes in a facet of child-specific executive function fluctuation (involving cognitive flexibility) among ten boys from Grade 4 (Yu et al., 2020). Participants completed between thirty-three and forty-three measurement occasions. Data were responses to a computerized short version of the Dimensional Change Card Sort task (Zelazo et al., 2013). Consistent with the Specificity Principle (Bornstein, 2019b), results (using dynamic structural equation modeling) demonstrated unique individual trajectories, which were not represented by the trajectory of group averages. More than half of the participants showed a negative association between executive functioning and inattention, but 20 percent showed a positive association between executive functioning and inattention.

These analyses demonstrated meaningful person-specific trajectories of executive functioning, suggesting that future study should undertake the analysis of individual development before data aggregation or generalization from aggregate statistics to individuals. The findings also demonstrate the usefulness of the Specificity Principle and the feasibility of collecting intensive longitudinal data to understand child development on an individual level as an alternative to immediate data aggregation. Simply, then, meaningful within-person variation exists over the course of a substantial portion of the school year.

Most "formative assessments" that teachers rely on in the school context are measured *once*, at the beginning of the year, and teachers use this single measure as an indicator of a student's present and even future abilities. At best, and in rare cases, variables involved in formative assessments are measured at three times across a school year. In effect, therefore, because of assessment practices in most school settings, the teacher must conclude that a student's score exists as a trait, as an index of a constant and contextually unalterable facet of a student's capacity or, at least, an attribute that teachers must try to maneuver slowly – like an aircraft carrier – over the course of the school year. However, the MMDC data show that a student cannot be and should not be defined by an initial measurement at the beginning of the year, and that, as emphasized throughout this Element, the variation in context and students' relation to the context, including their teachers, is associated with meaningful differences in their expression of BBFL characteristics across the school year.

If a teacher believes a single measure is equivalent to a trait (a facet of behavior presumed to be immutable) (McCrae et al., 2000) or worse, a marker of the potential of a child, then the onset of a teacher's behavior toward the child may be traced to the moment that this judgment is made. If this initial measurement happened on the day a child returns to school after being home with asthma or, as well, because of social isolation enacted due to the COVID-19 pandemic, this measurement – devoid of sensitivity to context – will provide an egregiously flawed appraisal of the child. However, the preliminary data from the MMDC project provide a counternarrative to this situation. These data reinforce the relative plasticity of children, and that change happens and can happen all the time in contexts that believe in, and are designed for, the growth and thriving of children.

In short, initial MMDC findings support the conclusions that children show meaningful individual pathways of skill development that cannot be adequately represented by aggregate data such as group averages. Of course, a key caveat to the MMDC findings at this writing is that we have studied these three foundational BBFL constructs *separately*. Within a dynamic, whole-child approach to studying child⟺context relations promoting thriving, the integrated study of these facets of development must be undertaken and further integrated with the study of BBFL constructs across tiers of the BBFL framework. Although considerable data indicate that these constructs coalesce – coact – within and across childhood (e.g., see McClelland et al., 2015), these findings are derived from variable-centered research. Accordingly, an essential next step in the child-specific work of the MMDC project is to study these coactions in child-specific manners across the tiers of the BBFL framework. We believe there will be several benefits of the continuation of generating and using child-specific measures in research and programs. These benefits will accrue in regard to the BBFL framework and to constructs associated with models of pathways for the development of academic competencies, resilience, or thriving in the face of adversity (e.g., Masten, 2014b; Spencer & Spencer, 2014; Spencer et al., 2015). Researchers and practitioners will have better knowledge of how specific children, living in specific contexts and having experienced specific life and traumatic events, may or may not develop crucial skills needed to cope and, even more, to thrive, no matter the context within which they are living during or after the pandemic.

3.8.1 MMDC and a Child-Specific Conceptualization of Whole-Child Development

Enhancing whole-child development and learning, and therefore the thriving of children, in schools and in out-of-school-settings, requires constructing and using measures that are able to detect changes in specific children, specific settings, and specific child⟺context relations. As we discussed in this Element, the conceptual and data analytic steps involved in accomplishing this work are complex but quite feasible. Even with the limitations involved in the initial stages of the MMDC research, it is clear that both change-sensitive measurements of development and change-sensitive analyses can be conducted. It is also clear that the specificity of change is evident. That is, as both Bornstein (2017, 2019b) and Rose (2016) pointed out, average developmental pathways do not adequately represent the variability in the individual pathways that are aggregated to constitute the average, and the individual data provide evidence of being meaningful, especially to professionals and practitioners across diverse fields. These findings suggest that there is reason to be optimistic that, in continuing MMDC research, stronger evidence will be provided for the conclusions drawn from the initial data we have summarized. Rather than defining such development through reference to averages, or on aggregated scores without evidence that they represent the meaningful pathways of the specific children involved in the computation of an average, whole-child development, learning, and thriving may be measured by studying what actually is happening in life – a continuous, bidirectional coaction with environments, experiences, and relationships across time.

In summary, the idea that an average score and single time of measurement can adequately represent the meaningful, specific attributes of an individual across time and place does not contribute to either good developmental science or to appropriate applications to education or to child-centered programming more generally. The interpretation that deviations from average scores mean that some children are in deficit and therefore in need of remediation contributes mightily to bad science, bad education, and bad child-centered programming.

The research and development work being undertaken within the SoLD Alliance has the potential to provide theory-predicated and methodologically rigorous evidence that child-specific (idiographic) tools can be used to understand specific pathways of specific children developing in specific settings (homes, schools, programs, neighborhoods). Such child-specific evidence can be used by researchers, educators, and child development practitioners to enhance their practice by placing a primary focus on the individuality and potential malleability of each individual. That is, the SoLD MMDC work is not intended to result only in tools for research. This work is aimed at transforming measurement in all learning and developmental settings, where context refers notably to homes, classrooms, and community-based programs. The language of measurement that we have introduced leads, therefore, to the new conceptualization of whole-child development, learning, and thriving as presented in this Element. This new conceptualization is discussed in detail in Section 4.

4 A New Conceptualization of Whole-Child Development, Learning, and Thriving

An embryo is formed by the combination of genetic and epigenetic contributions of two people. It is nurtured in the context of the womb and emerges as an infant. The infant is born, and the parents, with the resources they possess and the knowledge they have, will be part of a series of child⇔parent relations that will constitute the course of development for this unique being. They will do so without knowing how the story will end, but they know they must act to support this new life unfolding positively. They will not know the attributes of this being for a long time, or who their child will be in the future. Parents only know that they must nurture their offspring with all the resources they have to enable this life to thrive. These open-ended processes, which happen every day between parents and children around the world, are what dynamic systems and web-like processes are all about. However, they are not – but should be – the processes that govern the design, structure, purpose, and goals of education systems.

The creation of one whole child is directly contingent on a set of conditions and open-ended processes that could take place in schools, homes, communities, ballfields – everywhere that children grow and learn – *if* these environments were designed for whole-child development, learning, and thriving. Frankly, these steps are not all that different from a parent rearing a child. When we parent, we know that what we put in shapes what will come out. Parenting is the most prevalent example we have of an open-ended system (Bornstein, 2019a). What we take for granted in parenting – that what we put in shapes what will come out – is true in educational settings, too. This fact forces us to ask – what could be true if educational and learning settings were designed to nurture children's potential? This goal is not what twentieth century education was designed to meet, but it is what twenty-first century education can achieve.

Scientists and educators must use present-day knowledge about what is needed to nurture the development of a whole human being to design new education and learning systems and settings. The collective implications of the defining attributes of human development and learning (i.e., the role of context, embodiment, jaggedness, developmental range, epigenetics, etc.) and their dynamic relation to one another demand the adoption of a new world view about the purpose of education, designed as an open system to enable each child to know and reach their individual potential. The physicist and philosopher Kuhn (1970) would term the revisions in understanding the development and education of children a true *paradigm shift*. Thus far, we have created interventions and programs that have generated only incremental change, and only for some children. What we need now is a transformational paradigm shift.

Human development and the learning sciences tell us that development is an open-ended system, happening over time in many different places. While development is occurring, the brain is becoming increasingly integrated and connected, acquiring the ability to perform increasingly complex skills, and improving its ability to ascribe meaning to new experiences. Human development and learning sciences tell us how micro-developmental processes – the construction of new skills for "proximal processes" (Vygotsky, 1978) – integrate and converge with macro-developmental processes (larger-scale processes in which many constructive activities come together to form complex skills) and then stabilize, such that they can be applied to new contexts over time. This application means that, although people develop their competencies over the long term, critical learning occurs in shorter time horizons through an accumulation of diverse, context-dependent, nonlinear growth experiences that produce increasingly important skills, competencies, identities, and knowledge.

Within our dynamic conception, whole-child development, learning, and thriving emerge from the malleability, agency, and developmental range of a child, as they draw on available resources and build a web of relations and experiences across the settings of their life. The nature of these webs presents both opportunities and risks to development, but can, if well-designed and intentional, provide the foundation for the development of dynamic, complex skills that ultimately reveal the talent, passions, and potential of each child. The pathways will be diverse, and the patterns jagged. Nevertheless, throughout the developmental web of contexts, relationships and experiences will: (1) drive the expression of each child's genetic endowment and epigenetic attributes; (2) harness the malleability of their bodies and brains; and (3) nurture the fullest expression of what each child becomes. What is being asked of our education and learning systems is to use the knowledge we have today, which is captured in these developmental principles, to ignite these developmental and learning processes along positive trajectories for each and every child.

If educators and child-serving professionals: (1) understand that children possess a broad set of potentialities across multiple domains (e.g., physical health; mental health; complex social, emotional, and cognitive development; core academic skills and knowledge; positive identity formation; agency); and (2) recognize that each child is an integrated dynamic system with virtually infinite horizons of developmental range; and that (3) each attribute of the child is a subsystem with its own developmental range, *then*, several outcomes will occur. Educators and child-serving professionals will: (1) make daily practice and policy decisions to ensure that *all* the adults in *all* the environments that compose our education and learning systems will understand and address the sources and manifestations of institutionalized racism and white privilege; (2) establish the core features of integrated developmental and learning settings; (3) understand that the primary role of the adult is not to teach discrete skills, but to create opportunities for each child to want to bring parts of their interests, passions, talents, prior experiences, culture, and existing capabilities to bear; and (4) recognize that children make such efforts in order to master increasingly complex skills because they are engaged and motivated to do so.

Such settings are:

(1) Attuned to the presence of biological, psychological, and sociocultural (embodied) attributes of each child within each setting in life;

(2) Able to foster positive developmental relationships in all aspects and activities;

(3) Integrating multidimensional practices to describe, explain, and optimize the fullest expression of developmental range of the diverse set of attributes in children who can and are acting with agency in such environments;

(4) Oriented to create conditions of support and opportunities for growth within and, critically, across settings that capitalize on the malleability of the child and the variable and jagged pathways through which they will acquire increasingly complex skills and academic competencies;

(5) Able to capitalize on the specific strengths, and potential growth in the strengths, of each child to build the cognitive, social, emotional, metacognitive, and motivational skills and positive identity to enable the child to both influence their setting and positively adapt to new challenges, including transfer of skills to new settings;

(6) Able to address sources of institutionalized racial oppression, sexism, marginalization, stereotyping, and individual bias that, taken together, diminish the opportunities for positive identity formation and the expression of an individual child's developmental range and potential; and

(7) Aligned with the resources for positive growth found in communities, cultural assets, families, schools, child development programs, faith-based organizations, and athletics.

When such a web of environments and experiences is constructed by educators and community professionals, then each child's learning and healthy whole-child development will be optimized. In Section 5, we present examples of environments and experiences that, together, provide a blueprint for innovative settings designed to promote whole-child development, learning, and thriving.

5 A Blueprint for Setting Design: Promoting Whole-Child Development, Learning, and Thriving

Transformation of the twentieth century education using twenty-first century knowledge demands a profound change in the worldview of key figures (policymakers, philanthropists, practitioners, researchers, families, and more) whose decisions and actions determine the guardrails for changing education systems in America. The paradigm shift we propose in this Element challenges the purpose of twenty-first century education and its design, asking that we bring about a transformation toward an *open system* guided by principles of equity and informed by developmental and learning science, one that will encompass how children synthesize experiences across both formal and informal settings. Looked at this way, children's experiences in diverse family, community, and cultural settings carry enormous significance for children's identity formation and their acquisition of complex skills and capabilities that prepare them for learning, work, and life.

The current US K-12 system was designed as a *closed system* (e.g., see Farrington, 2020). Children come into school to learn. Teachers teach inside classrooms, make assessments, administer tests, and file reports. Children are moved forward (or not) in lockstep by grade. The classroom is thought to be the primary setting where learning happens. Other settings, even within the school, are not usually seen as places where learning and development happen; therefore, these settings are not staffed and resourced to promote learning experiences. They are often seen as places to keep children safe, fed, and motivated until they can return to learning in the classroom.

The potential learning value and capacities of these nonclassroom, and out-of-school-time learning settings are being underestimated. Such settings offer children opportunities for social exploration, personal discovery, and experimentation in ways that are not often possible in a formal classroom setting. In addition, partnerships that are formed with other systems offer the opportunity to connect children with nonacademic supports that children need to succeed. Overall, these experiences, in and out of formal school settings, could provide rich developmental activities of enormous significance to the broader purpose of schooling, learning, identity development, and thriving that we propose in this Element.

There are plentiful examples of individual schools, school systems, and innovative networks that have adopted versions of the principles we have advanced in this Element, including through the application of specific whole-child frameworks, such as the BBFL framework (Stafford-Brizard, 2016). In addition, we provide examples of programs, approaches, and tools that align with the scientific principles and a new purpose of twenty-first century education.

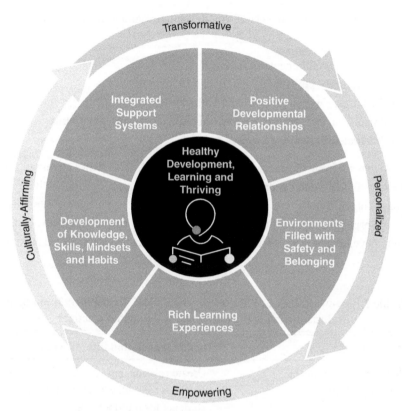

Figure 5 Guiding principles for equitable whole-child design
(from Darling-Hammond et al., 2020).

We present the following as a general framework for *operationalizing* whole-child development, learning, and thriving. This framework is derived from, and is intended to integrate, key seminal bodies of work specifically drawn from the literatures of thriving (e.g., Benson & Pittman, 2001; Lerner, 2004), human development (e.g., Bornstein & Leventhal, 2015), and education practice (e.g., Cantor et al., 2019; Darling-Hammond et al., 2020; Osher, Cantor, et al., 2020).

We have intentionally modified the framework and figure presented in Darling-Hammond et al. (2020) to allow for applicability to and beyond K-12 settings (see Figure 5). We retain the core design principles and elaborate crosscutting themes across all elements in the figure, but we have tried to present them in a form that creates opportunities for application of these design principles across the fields of early childhood, mental health, education, and developmental science. This presentation is intended to acknowledge the developmental continuum of optimizing experiences and relationships both in and out of formal school settings and across time.

The individual components of this developmental and learning framework are:

(1) Positive Developmental Relationships
(2) Environments Filled with Safety and Belonging
(3) Rich Learning Experiences and Pathways
(4) Intentional Development of Critical Skills, Mindsets, and Habits
(5) Integrated Systems of Support

Together, these elements support optimized development, learning, and thriving for all young people. Table 2 provides examples of innovative programs, organizations, and schools that have already applied these integrated design principles toward the goals of equity, wellness, academic growth, whole-child development, learning, and thriving. These examples are not exhaustive.

Table 2 Blue-wheel-based principles of whole-child development (see Figure 5): Instantiation in organizational and program practices

Principle	Possible translation into practice
Positive developmental relationships	• Create relationship-rich learning communities through educators staying with students for multiple years. • Mentoring relationships. • Learning about students' strengths and needs through check-ins, journaling, consistent family engagement.
Environments filled with safety and belonging	• Cocreated norms giving students ownership for their learning; fair, consistent, and predictable expectations and routines. • Creating explicitly anti-racist cultures; valuing and building on students' cultures and identities; eliminating implicit and explicit bias. • Coregulatory and restorative discipline practices aligned with school norms and culture.
Rich learning experiences and pathways	• Inquiry, problem-based, project-based, and collaborative learning opportunities promoting knowledge and skill development and transfer.

Table 2 (cont.)

Principle	Possible translation into practice
	• Formative teaching, assessment, and feedback providing students with consistent information about knowledge and skill development, personalized scaffolding, supports, and pathways managing their learning. • Integration of challenging academic content with explicit focus on developing knowledge, skills, mindsets, and habits for learning and development. • Students empowered to progress along their own learning pathways.
Intentional development of critical skills, mindsets, and habits	• Intentional instruction, modeling, and practice of knowledge, skills, mindsets, and habits for healthy learning and development, aligned to BBFL framework, integrated with instruction and learning of academic content. • Metacognitive language and modeling practices making learning and skill development visible to students.
Integrated systems of support	• Comprehensive, integrated, holistic, tiered support systems providing opportunities to pursue interests, extend learning, improve foundational skills, and address barriers to learning. • Supports that are culturally competent, developmentally appropriate, holistic, and asset-based.

Note 1: Websites of example organizations and programs: City Year: www.cityyear.org; Communities in Schools: www.communitiesinschools.org/; Ecological Approaches to Social Emotional Learning (EASEL) Laboratory: www.easel.gse.harvard.edu; EF +Math: www.efmathprogram.org; EL Education: www.eleducation.org.

Summit Learning: www.summitlearning.org; Transcend partnership with Van Ness ES: www.transcendeducation.org/blog-full; Transforming Education: www.transformingeducation.org; Turnaround for Children: www.turnaroundusa.org; Valor Collegiate Academies: www.valorcollegiate.org; Weikart Center for Youth Program Quality (a unit of the Forum for Youth Investment).

Note 2: To be effective, each of the guiding principles for whole-child learning must be transformative, personalized, empowering, and culturally-affirming.

They were chosen specifically for their grounding in the scientific and design principles presented in this Element.

Linda Darling-Hammond presents a complementary analysis of the key features of sustainable, scalable approaches to whole-child education in Box 5.

Linda Darling-Hammond

In the United States, progressive educators have long sought to transform schools in ways allowing more student-centered, inquiry-driven, community-connected approaches that nurture the whole child. From John Dewey, founder of the University of Chicago Laboratory School, to William A. Robinson, founder of the Atlanta University Laboratory School and an organizer of Black progressive educators in the South (Cremin, 1961), innovators have drawn on the sciences of learning and development as they evolved, along with their own close observations of children, to create schools that mirror the principles described in this Element.

Yet, sustaining and spreading these models have remained a challenge. Classrooms and schools that support strong, long-term relationships, student-centered learning, and strong community connections confront a wide range of institutional barriers. These barriers include the factory model school structures that depersonalized schools at the turn of the twentieth century; the textbooks and pacing guides that direct attention away from students' interests, cultural and community experiences, and zones of proximal development; and the testing and tracking systems that presume fixed intelligence along a bell curve, reinforcing discrimination based on race, economic status, and language background. Developing and retaining the "infinitely skilled teachers" who can support this kind of learning has also been a challenge in sustaining progressive education reform (Hernández et al., 2019).

Nevertheless, there are thousands of schools in the United States that have been redesigned to reflect student-centered principles, and many have now created networks that support professional development to deepen their work. Kridel (2018) showed how three of these high school networks create positive outcomes for students from marginalized racial, ethnic, and linguistic groups. The networks include:

- *Big Picture Learning*, whose experiential approach, grounded in personalized courses of study and workplace learning, typically takes place in community internships;
- *The Internationals Network for Public Schools*, serving new immigrant students through collaborative, inquiry-based learning for new English learners; and
- *New Tech Network*, which offers interdisciplinary project-based learning that is team-based and technology-supported.

All of the networks enable students to "learn how to learn" and develop the intrapersonal and interpersonal skills and mindsets that increase self-awareness, executive function, perseverance, and resilience. These developments are made possible through:

- advisory systems that enable small groups of students to work with the same advisor who supports their social, emotional, and academic needs over multiple years;
- teacher teams that share students and sometimes loop with them for more than one year, while collaborating on untracked curriculum that is interdisciplinary and project-based;
- restorative practices enabling strong, caring communities in which students preserve and strengthen relationships and supports for each other; and
- linkages to community organizations providing a range of wraparound supports as well as internships and authentic learning experiences.

The three networks have planted these sophisticated models in hundreds of other public schools across the United States by working closely with districts to engage communities; help educators and members of the public see and experience new models of education; co-construct new school structures along with pedagogies; develop knowledgeable leaders;

provide curriculum supports and ongoing training and coaching to teachers and other staff; and engage in continuous improvement. Although the work is difficult, these efforts show that it is not at all impossible (Kridel, 2018).

5.1 Implications of the Blueprint for Settings

The parable of the blind men touching the elephant is a useful metaphor for the examples shared above. Each example touches on different facets of our conception of whole-child design, some involving K-12 education and some involving out-of-school-time programs. As a consequence, each example still depicts a subset, not the entirety, of our full conception of whole-child design.

Nevertheless, across the examples, concepts from dynamic systems models that integrate relationships, dynamic skill development, and the constructive web are used. These examples reveal innovations that use dynamic systems concepts. These changes in the educational *zeitgeist* and the disruptions caused by COVID-19 and growing awareness of racism and racial inequity suggest that the time could be right for a transformational movement. The movement we envision will use the knowledge in this Element to create and evaluate holistic examples of whole-child education, systems of integrated school-family-community support, and anti-racist policies that celebrate each child's individual variation, jagged development, and specific developmental range. Together, these initiatives will create an increasing number of pathways through which each child can grow and thrive along positive life trajectories toward life success and fulfillment (Immordino-Yang et al., 2018).

Despite only touching different parts of the elephant, the dynamic systems-based vision for whole-child development, learning, and thriving that we present in this Element enables readers to see, touch, hear, and smell the *whole elephant* as it lives and develops. We hope that this vision of whole-child development, learning, and thriving will define a new twenty-first century approach to education and inspire innovations in design across diverse settings. These innovations will build on the assets, strengths, and potentials of each child; dismantle the institutional forces that hinder the growth of some children and holistically foster the growth of all children across the diverse communities; and optimize access to all forms of resources and opportunities. To realize this vision, we must apply innovations in child-specific measurement (Molenaar & Nesselroade, 2014, 2015; Rose, 2016). We need these innovations in measurement in scalable flexible forms to support educator practice attuned to children and to provide both the stories *and* the evidence of the effects of holistic, rigorous, and anti-racist approaches to human development and learning.

6 The Story We Have Told

Not everything that is faced can be changed, but nothing can be changed until it is faced.

James Baldwin (1962)

Here is what we are facing: It is not possible to talk proactively about the development, learning, and thriving of children without talking about opportunity, access, resources, and social capital. And it is not possible to talk productively about any of those things without talking about race and how it intersects with other issues, such as poverty, health, stereotype, and white privilege.

Our societal structures were designed to privilege some and not others. Our education systems were designed for sorting and selecting, based on beliefs and assumptions that we now know to be false, and that we have summarized in this Element. But these false assumptions are not the only drivers of the design of our public systems. US public systems, including our education systems, were intentionally and systematically designed to promote, privilege, and advantage specific groups, predominantly white, middle- to upper-class males, and to oppress and marginalize other ethnicities and genders. The institutional forces that have enabled this racist system to exist can be found in every corner of the social, economic, and educational infrastructure:

> Our society was built on the racial segmentation of personhood. Some people were full humans guaranteed non-enslavement, secured from expropriation and given the protection of law, and some people – Blacks, Natives and other nonwhites – were not. That unequal distribution of personhood was an economic reality as well. It shaped your access to employment and capital; determined whether you would be doomed to the margins or given access to its elevated ranks; marked who might share in the bounty of capitalist production and who would most likely be cast out as disposable. (Bouie, 2020, p. 1)

If the United States wanted to right the wrongs of today and the 400 years of policies and practices behind them, it would have to rethink systems based on the scientific principles presented in this Element. These principles tell an optimistic story about what is possible for children – their learning and their lives – when environments, experiences, and relationships are designed for development, health, learning, and access to opportunity and resources. Under these conditions, the potential that exists in each and every child has a much greater chance of being expressed, no matter where their journeys begin. The principles in this Element can serve as a guide to what we can do to optimize all children's learning and development and what we must stop doing now because it is actively harmful to the learning and development of many children. These actions include dismantling the institutions that preserve and sustain harmful, racist practices including tracking, harsh discipline, exclusion, shaming, and many others.

In this Element, we have explained that the twentieth century US education system was not designed based on knowledge of contemporary scholarship about human development and the learning sciences. It was never designed to develop the whole child. It was not designed for equity – to see students as individuals and to unleash the potential inside them. It was designed based on the belief that some children were more deserving of opportunity than others.

Education has reached the limit of what it can achieve through standardized and outdated approaches, as has happened in other fields. These approaches work for some – mainly those born into privilege – but not for many others. When other fields, such as health or medicine, hit a point where fundamental assumptions and beliefs needed to be challenged, this led to breakthrough solutions that benefited many more people.

For example, twenty-five years ago, cancer researchers were stuck using therapies that worked for some, but not others. When they asked themselves why, they recognized that they needed to understand more about the microenvironments around specific cancer cells so they could personalize individual treatments by building more targeted, context-sensitive therapies. This insight fueled new breakthroughs in cancer treatments, enabling doctors to successfully treat far more patients. It also led to the creation of a new field – immunotherapy – where an individual's own immune system is recruited to fight a cancer.

In this example, a standardized approach to treatment was disrupted and moved to a *personalized* approach. This pattern – disruption of standardization leading to personalization – has also transformed other fields and industries (e.g., the travel and media industries). Examples include travel through Airbnb, music through Spotify, and entertainment through Netflix.

This kind of transformational shift must now happen in education and child development. We envision a system that is personalized so that it can see all children as individuals, one that recognizes children's specific assets, strengths, and vulnerabilities and that uses this child-specific knowledge to influence the design of environmental contexts and individual⇔context relations that support learning, meaning-making, identity development, and thriving as individuals (e.g., see Spencer, 2006; Spencer et al., 2015).

To achieve the transformation needed today, education systems must be willing to embrace what is known about how children learn and develop. The core message from diverse sciences is clear: The range of students' skills and knowledge – and, ultimately, students' potential as human beings – can be significantly influenced through exposure to highly favorable conditions. Such conditions involve learning environments and experiences that are intentionally designed to optimize student-specific development (Bloom, 1984; Fischer & Bidell, 2006). To create this transformation, the scientific principles highlighted in this Element must become the foundation for new twenty-first century education and learning systems designed around the acquisition of twenty-first century skills and mastery-level competencies.

With what we know today, we can design environments that help protect children from developmental harm, including racist policies and behaviors, and promote their healthy development and success as learners. The nonnegotiable features described in this Element will simultaneously ignite brain development and learning, promote well-being, support positive identity formation, enable the acquisition of knowledge, skills, and mindsets that are critical for success in learning and work, build resilience to future stressors, and provide the intellectual challenge and rigor that will enable children to formulate the specific personal, academic, and social goals they desire to achieve and are capable of attaining under the right conditions. Settings designed in these ways will provide a developmental continuum of experiences, both in and out of school, and across age bands, that optimize each student's developmental range and unveil the talent, skills, and potential that all children have.

In the design process, we can ask and answer the same question that cancer researchers asked: What can we do that will work optimally for this specific child in this specific context? This question will move scientists and educators to fundamentally different answers about the way schools and education systems of the future must be designed – toward integrated and individualized processes and supports, using tools and platforms that enable educators to integrate academic instruction with the intentional development of the skills and mindsets that all successful learners have.

Breakthroughs do not occur when we seek to achieve them by doing what we have been doing, just a little better. The approaches we have been taking thus far to learning and schools have not fully challenged our assumptions about talent – is it plentiful or scarce; about human skills – are they malleable or are they fixed; or about human potential – what is any child capable of under the right conditions?

In this Element, we have presented the scientific basis for a profound shift away from the assumptions and practices that have dominated twentieth century education. Building highly favorable conditions into all of the environments in which children grow and learn will put many children on the path to equity and thriving and all children on the path to the fullest expression of their potential.

The message in the science is so optimistic: Genes are chemical followers. Context shapes the expression of our genetic attributes. This is the biologic truth. Schools designed, as Bloom (1984) described, using the levers of human development – so that what one child can do, nearly all children can do under highly favorable conditions – can be our new twenty-first century learning and development system: A system designed to see and unleash talent and potential and ensure that all children can thrive. This vision constitutes a transformational shift in the purpose and potential of education, a dismantling of the systems that constrain this vision, grounded in what we know *today* about human development, the development of the brain, and learning science.

7 Toward the New Story that Must Be Told

Around the world, children's life chances are still defined largely by where they live (by a zip code in the United States). Zip code often dictates which schools children can attend and the quality of those schools; the quality of housing, food, and water supply; access to high-quality healthcare; and the depth of community resources that exist to support families (e.g., Sampson, 2016). Adults and children in low-income communities with large populations of individuals of color have experienced centuries of injustice due to systemic and institutional racism and oppression – including racist housing practices, education, healthcare, and economic policies; police brutality; and marginalization – causing high levels of adversity and persistent stress, which compromise community well-being (e.g., Galea et al., 2020; Murry et al., 2015). COVID-19 and the economic destabilization it has caused, coupled with rising attention to police brutality and resulting societal unrest, compound existing inequities and create profound challenges to family and community stability, in particular for Black and brown children and families (e.g., Fortuna et al., 2020).

Looked at through the lens of the concepts presented in this Element, these issues of adversity and inequity are becoming the defining features of the context in which many millions of children in the United States are growing up (at the time we are writing this Element). This situation presents a significant risk to the United States: A growing percentage of the current generation of children could now, and moving forward, be living life on an expanding economic, educational, developmental, and social precipice. Winthrop (2018) explained that, by 2030, there will be 800 million children who will have reached their adulthood without possessing basic secondary level skills. Winthrop believes that a century of progress is needed to enable most marginalized children to attain the sort of education that the wealthiest children experience at this writing.

Although these risks are not new, they are becoming more pronounced in the form of inequitable hardship and higher barriers to quality education and jobs, with shrinking opportunities for economic and social mobility (Ambrose, 2020; Fortuna et al., 2020). Furthermore, due to the new realities that COVID-19 has created, children and families who had surmounted barriers and secured access to high-quality education and jobs, who had managed to move out of poverty, are being pushed back into positions of insecurity and risk, with college education, high-paying jobs, and housing security increasingly out of reach (e.g., Patel et al., 2020).

We are facing an impending convergence of several long-standing, but exacerbated realities that will threaten the economy of the United States for years to come and compromise the futures of specific subpopulations in particular (e.g., Blundell et al., 2020). There is a growing gap in opportunity and life outcomes in specific subgroups, for example between students in wealthy, working-class communities and students in low-income urban and rural districts, especially students of color, whose circumstances have now been rendered significantly more challenging. Poverty among US children exists at an alarming rate (Koball & Jiang, 2018).

The United States is seeing declining performance and opportunity at both ends of the achievement spectrum. At the higher end, US students are declining in their performance on the Programme for International Student Assessment (PISA) test as compared to students in other industrialized nations (e.g., Darling-Hammond, 2014). This change reveals a risk that US students will not be as qualified for the world's most competitive and desirable job opportunities as students from other countries (OCED, 2019; Tucker, 2020a, 2020b). Looking beyond these statistics reveals that education and teaching have not universally been incorporating recent findings from neuroscience and the learning sciences and have not sufficiently emphasized the breadth of skills, or what some refer to as twenty-first century skills, that prioritize how to use knowledge and the interpersonal and intrapersonal skills needed to thrive in work, citizenship, and life (Winthrop, 2018).

The performance of US students in the bottom half of achievement distributions has also continued to decline, with clear parallels to other societal metrics including child poverty rates and the highly inequitable allocations of per-pupil funding for education across states and districts (Koball & Jiang, 2018). These trends began before COVID-19 and can be expected to worsen given the pandemic context. But perhaps the greatest risk to students at the lower end of the distribution is that their education has never focused on the acquisition of twenty-first century deeper learning skills, which means they will be at far greater risk from the consequences of the COVID-19 pandemic. The education that they received pre-pandemic never prepared them with the breadth of skills to adapt to manifold changes in society and the demands of the workplace, but instead placed a narrow focus on specific types of content acquisition. When we ask the question – what tools in our adaptive kit will any of us use to navigate massive changes in the way we live and work? – we realize that they are our agency, our problem-solving skills, our abilities to collaborate with others, our creativity, and our resilience. In other words, it is a twenty-first century toolkit of skills that we will call upon.

As the United States seeks to expand the use of artificial intelligence (AI) and to reduce health risks by further automatizing and robotizing jobs, its citizens may face dramatic reductions in job opportunities for young and/or less skilled adults who have graduated from high school and engaged in some postsecondary education and employment (e.g., Furman & Seamans, 2019). This trend creates a significant risk that an increasing number of young adults will face crippling challenges due to economic hardship, a dearth of especially well-paying jobs, an inability to pursue further education, and the challenge of adequately supporting a young family's basic needs (e.g., Huang & Rust, 2018).

To the extent we believe that this set of changes will affect only some of us, but not others – we are wrong. These changes are happening quickly all around us and will affect the United States and its prospects for growth, prosperity, and well-being for years to come. Before the COVID-19 pandemic, Chetty et al. (2020) showed that children born in 1940 had a 90 percent chance of earning more than their parents, but for children born four decades later, that chance had fallen to 50 percent. What would those numbers be today? Right now, we are seeing a picture where the children of the wealthy will increasingly acquire these adaptive twenty-first century skills within schools that specifically prioritize such achievements and poor children will still be attending schools that are not resourced to develop this full set of skills and where the acquisition of literacy and math skills will be the benchmark of success. The magnitude of the gap that derives from this disparity is profound in its implications.

The forces shaping and challenging children's futures before the pandemic and the social and economic crises of 2020 and 2021 have dramatically amplified the manifestations of inequity of educational experiences among children across the United States and the world. These forces cry out for an examination of specific factors that could accelerate genuine opportunity for children, families, and communities versus factors that will continue to condemn them to joblessness, homelessness, and stagnation. Such positive factors include educational opportunities and experiences that do not fall prey to false choices between core academic skills and competencies and the acquisition of robust twenty-first century skills and social capital. They also include educational and community contexts designed to meet basic needs and provide the tools for adaptation, innovation, and personal growth.

The advent of precision medicine, which changed the medical field and practice, began with accepting individual variability and seeks to analyze disease processes simultaneously through genetic, environmental, and biologic lenses to more accurately predict which combination of prevention and intervention strategies will be successful for a specific patient with a specific malady at a specific moment in time. We believe there is a social analog to precision medicine in the biological, genetic, developmental, and learning principles described in this Element. The enactment of these principles could lead to a substantial redesign of developmental, learning, and measurement systems that educate and empower individual children, if such change stays focused on the agency and self-constructive skills of children to be active producers of their positive futures. Possessing the full set of twenty-first century skills and mastery-level competencies, coupled with access to social capital and opportunity, and then measurement systems to further empower transformational change, could render this vision a reality.

The truth is that reimagining schools and systems to address structural inequities will benefit everyone. The contexts that drive inequity and despair for families and communities result from being denied the opportunities and resources needed to thrive. When we create schools and communities designed for greater equity and opportunity, we will help all families experiencing social and economic pressures see a pathway toward stabilization, opportunity, and thriving.

Indeed, the forces of 2020 can and should serve as an inflection point for instigating and empowering transformational societal, educational, and economic change, defined by the goals of social justice, multidimensional equity, economic opportunity, and human thriving for each and every child (Cantor & Osher, in press; Osher, Pittman, et al., 2020).

References

Allport, G. W. (1937). *Personality: A psychological interpretation*. New York, NY: Holt.

Allport, G. W. (1968). *The person in psychology: Selected essays*. Boston, MA: Beacon Press.

Ambrose, A. J. H. (2020). Inequities during COVID-19. *Pediatrics, 146*(2), e20201501. https://doi.org/10.1542/peds.2020-1501

Anderson, R. E., McKenny, M., & Mitchell, A. (2018). EMBRacing racial stress and trauma: Preliminary feasibility and coping responses of a racial socialization intervention. *Journal of Black Psychology, 44*(1), 25–46.

Bailey, R., Meland, E. A., Brion-Meisels, G., & Jones, S. M. (2019). Getting developmental science back into schools: Can what we know about self-regulation help change how we think about "No Excuses"? *Frontiers in Psychology, 10*(01885), 1–15. https://doi.org/10.3389/fpsyg.2019.01885

Baldwin, J. (1962). As much truth as one can bear, New York Times Book Review, January 14, 120, 148.

Baltes, P. B., Lindenberger, U., & Staudinger, U. M. (2006). Life span theory in developmental psychology. In R.M. Lerner (ed.), *Theoretical models of human development. Handbook of child psychology* (Vol. 1, 6th ed., pp.569–664). Hoboken, NJ: John Wiley & Sons.

Bateson, P. & Gluckman, P. (2011). *Plasticity, development and evolution*. Cambridge, UK: Cambridge. https://doi.org/10.1093/ije/dyr240

Benson P. L. & Pittman, K. J. (eds.). (2001). *Trends in youth development: Visions, realities and challenges*. Boston, MA: Kluwer Academic Publishers. https://doi.org/10.1007/978-1-4615-1459-6

Bernstein, B. E., Meissner, A., & Lander, E. S. (2007). The mammalian epigenome. *Cell, 128*(4), 669–81. https://doi.org/10.1016/j.cell.2007.01.033

Blair, C. & Ursache, A. (2011). A bidirectional model of executive functions and self-regulation. In R.F. Baumeister & K. D. Vohs (eds.), *Handbook of self-regulation* (2nd ed., pp. 300–20). New York, NY: Guilford Press.

Bloom, B. S. (1984). The 2 Sigma problem: The search for methods of group instruction as effective as one-to-one tutoring. *Educational Researcher, 13*(6), 4–16. https://doi.org/10.3102/0013189X013006004

Bloom, B. S. (ed.). (1985). *Developing talent in young people*. New York: Ballantine Books.

Blundell, R., Costa Dias, M., Joyce, R., & Xu, X. (2020). COVID-19 and inequalities. *Fiscal Studies, 41*(2), 291–319. https://doi.org/10.1111/1475-5890.12232

Bogard, K., Murry, V. M., & Alexander, C. (eds.) (2017). *Perspectives on health equity & social determinants of health.* Washington, DC: National Academy of Medicine.

Boldrini, M., Placidi, G., & Marazziti, D. (1998). Applications of chaos theories to psychiatry: A review and future perspectives. *CNS Spectrums, 3*(1), 22–9. https://doi.org/10.1017/S1092852900005356

Bornstein, M. H. (2017). The specificity principle in acculturation science. *Perspectives in Psychological Science, 12*(1), 3–45. https://doi.org/10.1177/1745691616655997

Bornstein, M. H. (ed.). (2019a). *Handbook of parenting.* Abington, UK: Routledge.

Bornstein, M. H. (2019b). Fostering optimal development and averting detrimental development: Prescriptions, proscriptions, and specificity. *Applied Developmental Science, 23*(4), 340–5. https://doi.org/10.1080/10888691.2017.1421424

Bornstein, M. H. & Leventhal, T. (2015). (eds.). *Ecological settings and processes. Handbook of child psychology and developmental science* (Vol. 4, 7th ed.). Editor-in-chief: R. M. Lerner Hoboken, NJ: Wiley.

Bornstein, M. H. & Putnick, D. L. (2019). *The architecture of the child mind: g, Fs, and the hierarchical model of intelligence.* New York: Routledge. https://doi.org/10.4324/9780429027307

Bornstein, M. H., Putnick, D. L., & Esposito, G. (2017). Continuity and stability in development. *Child Development Perspectives, 11*(2), 113–19. https://doi.org/10.1111/cdep.12221

Bouie, J. (2020). "Beyond 'white fragility'." *The New York Times*, June 26. www.nytimes.com/2020/06/26/opinion/blackBlack-lives-matter-injustice.html

Brackett, M. A., Elbertson, N. A., & Rivers, S. E. (2015). Applying theory to the development of approaches to SEL. In J. A. Durlak, C. E. Domitrovich, R. P. Weissberg, & T. P. Gullotta (eds.), *Handbook of social and emotional learning: Research and practice* (pp. 20–32). New York: The Guilford Press.

Bronfenbrenner, U. & Morris, P. A. (2006). The bioecological model of human development. In W. Damon & R.M. Lerner (eds.) & R. M. Lerner (Vol. ed.), *Theoretical models of human development. Handbook of child psychology* (Vol. 1, 6th ed., pp. 793–828). Hoboken, NJ: John Wiley & Sons.

Burt, C. (1966). The genetic determination of differences in intelligence: A study of monozygotic twins reared together and apart. *British Journal of Psychology, 57*, 137–53. https://doi.org/10.1111/j.2044-8295.1966.tb01014.x

Cantor, P. (2020). Keynote address: Whole child development: Dynamics of trauma, stress, and learning. Learning and the Brain Conference. San Francisco, CA, February 14–16.

Cantor, P. & Osher, D. (in press). *The science of learning and development.* New York: Routledge.

Cantor, P., Osher, D., Berg, J., Steyer, L. & Rose, T. (2019). Malleability, plasticity, and individuality: How children learn and develop in context. *Applied Developmental Science, 23*(4), 307–37. https://doi.org/10.1080/10888691.2017.1398649

Chetty, R., Hendren, N., Jones, M. R., & Porter, S. R. (2020). Race and economic opportunity in the United States: An intergenerational perspective. *Quarterly Journal of Economics, 135*(2), 711–83. https://doi.org/10.1093/qje/qjz042

Cremin, L. A. (1961). *The transformation of the school: Progressivism in American education, 1876–1957.* New York: Knopf.

Csikszenthihalyi, M. & Rathunde, K. (1998). The development of the person: An experiential perspective on the ontogenesis of psychological complexity. In R. M. Lerner (ed.), *Theoretical models of human development. Handbook of child psychology.* (Vol. 1, 6th ed., pp. 635–84). Editors-in-chief: R. M. Lerner and W. Damon. New York: Wiley.

Csikszentmihalyi, M., Rathunde, K., & Whalen, S. (1993). *Talented teenagers: The roots of success and failure.* New York: Cambridge University Press.

Darling-Hammond, L. (2014). What can PISA tell us about U.S. education policy? *New England Journal of Public Policy, 26*(1), Article 4, 1–14.

Darling-Hammond, L., Flook, L., Cook-Harvey, C., Barron, B., & Osher, D. (2020). Implications for educational practice of the science of learning and development. *Applied Developmental Science, 24*(2), 97–140. https://doi.org/10.1080/10888691.2018.1537791

Darwin, C. (1859). *The origin of species by means of natural selection or the preservation of favoured races in the struggle for life.* London: J. Murray. https://doi.org/10.5962/bhl.title.68064

Darwin, C. (1872). *The expression of emotions in man and animals.* London: J. Murray. https://doi.org/10.1037/10001-000

Dawson, T. L. (2020). Rethinking educational assessment in light of a strong theory of development. In M. F. Mascolo & T. R. Bidell (eds.), *Handbook of integrative developmental science: Essays in honor of Kurt W. Fischer* (pp. 423–50). New York: Routledge. https://doi.org/10.4324/9781003018599-17

Dweck, C. (2016). *Mindset: The new psychology of success.* New York: Ballantine.

Elder, G. H., Jr. (1998). The life course and human development. In W. Damon (Series ed.) & R. M. Lerner (Vol. ed.), *Theoretical models of human development. Handbook of child psychology* (Vol. 1, 5th ed., pp. 939–91). New York: Wiley.

Elder, G. H., Jr., Shanahan, M. J., & Jennings, J. A. (2015). Human development in time and place. *Handbook of Child Psychology and Developmental Science, 4,* 1–49. https://doi.org/10.1002/9781118963418.childpsy402

Emmerich, W. (1968). Personality development and concepts of structure. *Child Development 39,* 671–90. https://doi.org/10.2307/1126978

Erikson, E. H. (1959). Identity and the life cycle. *Psychological Issues, 1,* 50–100.

Eysenck, H. J. (1979). Genetic models, theory of personality and the unification of psychology. In J. R. Royce & L. P. Mos (eds.), *Theoretical advances in behavior genetics* (pp. 517–40). Rockville, MD: Sijthoff and Noordhoff. https://doi.org/10.1007/978-94-009-8576-6_15

Farrington, C. A. (2020). Equitable learning and development: Applying science to foster liberatory education. *Applied Developmental Science, 24*(2), 159–69. https://doi.org/10.1080/10888691.2019.1609730

Fass, P. S. (1991). *Outside in: Minorities and the transformation of American education.* New York: Oxford University Press.

Felitti, V. J., Anda, R. F., Nordenberg, D., et al. (1998). Relationship of childhood abuse and household dysfunction to many of the leading causes of death in adults: The Adverse Childhood Experiences (ACE) Study. *American Journal of Preventive Medicine, 14*(4), 245–58.

Fischer, K. W. & Bidell, T. R. (2006). Dynamic development of action and thought. In R. M. Lerner (ed.). *Theoretical models of human development. Handbook of child psychology* (Vol 1, 6th ed., pp. 313–99). Editors-in-chief: W. Damon & R. M. Lerner. Hoboken, NJ: Wiley. https://doi.org/10.1002/dvdy.20917

Fischer, K. W., Rose, L.T., & Rose, S. (2007). Growth cycles of mind and brain: Analyzing developmental pathways of learning disorders. In K. W. Fischer, J. H. Bernstein, & M. H. Immordino-Yang (eds.), *Mind, brain, & education in reading disorders.* New York: Cambridge University Press.

Fortuna, L. R., Tolou-Shams, M., Robles-Ramamurthy, B., & Porche, M. V. (2020). Inequity and the disproportionate impact of COVID-19 on communities of color in the United States: The need for a trauma-informed social justice response. *Psychological Trauma: Theory, Research, Practice, and Policy, 12*(5), 443–5. https://doi.org/10.1037/tra0000889

Freedle, R. (1977). Psychology, Thomian topologies, deviant logics, and human development. In N. Datan & H. W. Reese (eds.), *Life-span developmental psychology: Dialectical perspectives on experimental research* (pp. 317–41). New York: Academic Press. https://doi.org/10.1016/B978-0-12-203560-9.50024-4

Furman, J. & Seamans, R. (2019). AI and the Economy. *Innovation Policy and the Economy, 19,* 161–91. https://doi.org/10.1086/699936

Galea, S., Merchant, R. M., & Lurie, N. (2020). The mental health consequences of COVID-19 and physical distancing: The need for prevention and early intervention. *JAMA Internal Medicine, 180*(6), 817–18. https://doi.org/10.1001/jamainternmed.2020.1562

Gottlieb, G. (1998). Normally occurring environmental and behavioral influences on gene activity: From central dogma to probabilistic epigenesis. *Psychological Review, 105*, 792–802. https://doi.org/10.1037/0033-295X.105.4.792-802

Gould, S. J. (1996). *The mismeasure of man* (revised/expanded ed.). New York: Norton.

Gould, S. J. & Vrba, E. S. (1982). Exaptation – a missing term in the science of form. *Paleobiology, 8*(1), 4–15. https://doi.org/10.1017/S0094837300004310

Granott, N. (2020). The puzzle of microdevelopment: Variability, fractals, and why developmental change is so different and still the same. In M. F. Mascolo & T. R. Bidell (eds.), *Handbook of integrative developmental science: Essays in honor of Kurt W. Fischer* (pp. 279–307). New York: Routledge. https://doi.org/10.4324/9781003018599-11

Halfon, N. & Forrest, C. B. (2018). The emerging theoretical framework of life course health development. In N. Halfon, C. B. Forrest, R. M. Lerner, & E. Faustman (eds.), *Handbook of life course health development* (pp 19–43). New York: Springer. https://doi.org/10.1007/978-3-319-47143-3_2

Halfon, N., Forrest, C. B., Lerner, R. M., & Faustman, E. (eds.) (2018). *Handbook of life course health development.* New York: Springer. https://doi.org/10.1007/978-3-319-47143-3

Hardway, C. (2020). Of interest and engagement: The emotional force of learning and development. In M. F. Mascolo & T. R. Bidell (eds.), *Handbook of integrative developmental science* (pp. 232–61). New York: Routledge.

Harper, L. V. (2005). Epigenetic inheritance and the intergenerational transfer of experience. *Psychological Bulletin, 131*, 340–60. https://doi.org/10.1037/0033-2909.131.3.340

Hebb, D. O. (1949). *The organization of behavior.* New York: Wiley.

Hebb, D. O. (1955). Drives and the C. N. S. (conceptual nervous system). *Psychological Review, 62*(4), 243–54. https://doi.org/10.1037/h0041823

Hernández, L. E., Darling-Hammond, L., Adams, J., & Bradley, K. (with Duncan Grand, D., Roc, M., & Ross, P.). (2019). *Deeper learning networks: Taking student-centered learning and equity to scale.* Palo Alto, CA: Learning Policy Institute. https://learningpolicyinstitute.org/product/deeper-learning-networks-report

Hinton, A. L., Woolford, A., & Benvenuto, J. (eds.). (2014). *Colonial genocide in indigenous North America*. Durham, NC: Duke University Press. https://doi.org/10.1215/9780822376149

Ho, M. W. & Saunders, P. T. (eds.). (1984).Beyond neo-Darwinism: An epigenetic approach to evolution. *Journal of Theoretical Biology, 78,* 573–91. https://doi.org/10.1016/0022-5193(79)90191-7

Huang, M-H. & Rust, R. T. (2018). Artificial Intelligence in service. *Journal of Service Research, 21*(2), 155–72. https://doi.org/10.1177/1094670517752459

Hubbard, R. & Wald, E. (1999). *Exploding the gene myth: How genetic information is produced and manipulated by scientists, physicians, employers, insurance companies, educators, and law enforcers*. Boston, MA: Beacon Press.

Immordino-Yang, M. H. (2016). Emotion, sociality, and the brain's default mode network: Insights for educational practice and policy. *Policy Insights from the Behavioral and Brain Sciences, 3*(2), 211–19. https://doi.org/10.1177/2372732216656869

Immordino-Yang, M. H. & Damasio, A. (2007). We feel, therefore we learn: The relevance of affective neuroscience to education. *Mind, Brain, and Education, 1*(1), 3–10. https://doi.org/10.1111/j.1751-228X.2007.00004.x

Immordino-Yang, M. H. & Knecht, D. R. (2020). Building meaning builds teens' brains. *Educational Leadership, 77*(8), 36–43.

Immordino-Yang, M. H. & Yang, X.-F. (2017). Cultural differences in the neural correlates of social–emotional feelings: An interdisciplinary, developmental perspective. *Current Opinion in Psychology, 17,* 34–40. https://doi.org/10.1016/j.copsyc.2017.06.008

Immordino-Yang, M. H., Darling-Hammond, L., & Krone, C. (2018). *The brain basis for integrated social, emotional, and academic development: How emotions and social relationships drive learning*. Washington, DC: The Aspen Institute.

Immordino-Yang, M. H., Darling-Hammond, L., & Krone, C. R. (2019). Nurturing nature: How brain development is inherently social and emotional, and what this means for education. *Educational Psychologist, 54*(3), 185–204. https://doi.org/10.1080/00461520.2019.1633924

Jablonka, E. & Lamb, M. (2005). *Evolution in four dimensions: Genetic, epigenetic, behavioral, and symbolic variation in the history of life*. Cambridge, MA: MIT Press.

Jones, S. M. & Kahn, J. (2017). *The evidence base for how we learn: Supporting students' social, emotional, and academic development*. National

Commission on Social, Emotional, and Academic Development Aspen Institute. Retrieved from: https://assets.aspeninstitute.org/content/uploads/2017/09/SEAD-Research-Brief-11.1.17.pdf

Joseph, J. (2015). *The trouble with twin studies: A reassessment of twin research in the social and behavioral sciences.* New York: Routledge. https://doi.org/10.4324/9781315748382

Keating, D. P. (2016). Transformative role of epigenetics in child development research: Commentary on the Special Section. *Child Development, 87*(1), 135–42.

Keller, E. F. (2010). *The mirage of a space between nature and nurture.* Durham, NC: Duke University Press. https://doi.org/10.1215/9780822392811

Kendi, I. X. (2019). *How to be an Anti-Racist.* New York: One World/Random House.

Kluckhohn, C. & Murray, H. (1948). (eds.), *Personality in nature, society, and culture.* New York: Knopf.

Koball, H. & Jiang, Y. (2018). *Basic facts about low-income children: Children under 18 years, 2016.* New York: National Center for Children in Poverty, Columbia University Mailman School of Public Health.

Knight, C. C. & Fischer, K. W. (1992). Learning to read words: Individual differences in developmental sequences. *Journal of Applied Developmental Psychology, 13*, 377–404. https://doi.org/10.1016/0193-3973(92)90037-I

Kridel, C. (ed.) (2018). *Becoming an African American progressive educator. Narratives from 1940s Black progressive high schools.* Columbia, SC: Museum of Education, University of South Carolina, Craig Kridel. www.museumofeducation.info/narratives.pdf

Kuhn, T. S. (1970). *The structure of scientific revolutions, 2nd ed.* Chicago, IL: University of Chicago Press.

Laceulle, O. M., Rentfrow, J., Lamb, M. E., & Alisic, E. (2019). General risk or individual vulnerability? Individual differences in young adult's health risk behavior after childhood trauma. *Personality and Individual Differences, 142*, 288–94. https://doi.org/10.1016/j.paid.2018.09.017

Lee, C. D. (2010). Soaring above the clouds, delving the ocean's depths: Understanding the ecologies of human learning and the challenge for education science. *Educational Researcher, 39*(9), 643–55. https://doi.org/10.3102/0013189X10392139

Lee, C. D. (2017). Integrating research on how people learn and learning across settings as a window of opportunity to address inequality in educational processes and outcomes. *Review of Research in Education, 41*(1), 88–111. https://doi.org/10.3102/0091732X16689046

Lee, C. D., Nasir, N. S., Pea, R., & deRoyston, M. (2020). Introduction. Reconceptualizing learning: A critical task for knowledge-building and teaching. In Nasir, N., Lee, C., Pea, R., & McKinney deRoyston (eds.), *Handbook of the cultural foundations of learning* (pp. xvii–xxxv). New York: Routledge. https://doi.org/10.4324/9780203774977

Lerner, R. M. (1984). *On the nature of human plasticity.* New York: Cambridge University Press. https://doi.org/10.1017/CBO9780511666988

Lerner, R. M. (1992). *Final solutions: Biology, prejudice, and genocide.* University Park: Penn State Press.

Lerner, R. M. (2004). *Liberty: Thriving and civic engagement among America's youth.* Thousand Oaks, CA: Sage Publications.

Lerner, R. M. (2012). Essay review. Developmental science: Past, present, and future. *International Journal of Developmental Science, 6*(1–2), 29–36. https://doi.org/10.3233/DEV-2012-12102

Lerner, R. M. (2018). *Concepts and theories of human development* (4th ed.). New York: Routledge. https://doi.org/10.4324/9780203581629

Lerner, R. M. & Overton, W. F. (2017). Reduction to absurdity: Why epigenetics invalidates all models involving genetic reduction. *Human Development, 60*(2–3), 107–23. https://doi.org/10.1159/000477995

Lerner, R. M., Lerner, J. V., Bowers, E., & Geldhof, G. J. (2015). Positive youth development and relational developmental systems. In W. F. Overton & P. C. Molenaar (eds.), *Theory and method. Handbook of child psychology and developmental science* (Vol 1, 7th ed., pp. 607–51). Editor-in-chief: R. M. Lerner. Hoboken, NJ: Wiley. https://doi.org/10.1002/9781118963418.childpsy116

Lewallen, T. C., Hunt, H., Potts-Datema, W., Zaza, S., & Giles, W. (2015). The whole school, whole community, whole child model: A new approach for improving educational attainment and healthy development for students. *Journal of School Health, 85*(11), 729–39. https://doi.org/10.1111/josh.12310

Lewontin, R. C., Rose, S., & Kamin, L. J. (1984). *Not in our genes: Biology, ideology, and human nature.* New York: Pantheon Press.

Li, J. (2020). The cultural framing of development. In M. F. Mascolo & T. R. Bidell (eds.), *Handbook of integrative developmental science: Essays in honor of Kurt W. Fischer* (pp. 308–22). New York: Routledge. https://doi.org/10.4324/9781003018599-12

Li, J. & Julian, M. M. (2012). Developmental relationships as the active ingredient: A unifying working hypothesis of "what works" across intervention settings. *American Journal of Orthopsychiatry, 82*(2), 157–66. https://doi.org/10.1111/j.1939-0025.2012.01151.x

Lorenz, K. (1940). Durch Domestikation verursachte Störungen arteigenen Verhaltens. *Zeitschrift für angewandte Psychologie und Charakterkunde, 59*, 2–81.

Lorenz, K. (1966). *On aggression.* New York: Harcourt, Brace & World.

Mascolo, M. F. & Bidell, T. R. (eds.). (2020). *Handbook of integrative developmental science: Essays in honor of Kurt W. Fischer.* New York: Routledge. https://doi.org/10.4324/9781003018599

Mascolo, M. F. & Fischer, K. W. (2015) Dynamic development of thinking, feeling, and acting. In W. F. Overton & P. C. Molenaar (eds.), *Theory and method. Handbook of child psychology and developmental science* (Vol 1, 7th ed., pp. 113–61). Editor-in-chief: R. M. Lerner. Hoboken, NJ: Wiley. https://doi.org/10.1002/9781118963418.childpsy104

Masten, A. S. (2007). Resilience in developing systems: Progress and promise as the fourth wave rises. *Development and Psychopathology, 19*(3), 921–30. https://doi.org/10.1017/S0954579407000442

Masten, A. S. (2014a). Invited commentary: Positive youth development and human complexity. *Journal of Youth and Adolescence, 43*, 1012–17. https://doi.org/10.1007/s10964-014-0124-9

Masten, A. S. (2014b). *Ordinary magic: Resilience in development.* New York: Guilford Press.

Masten, A. S. , Narayan, A. J., Silverman, W. K., & Osofsky, J. D. (2015). Children in war and disaster. In M. H. Bornstein and T. Leventhal (eds.), *Ecological settings and processes. Handbook of child psychology and developmental science* (Vol. 4, 7th ed., pp. 704–45). Editor-in-chief: R. M. Lerner. Hoboken, NJ: Wiley.

McAdoo, H. P. (1999). Diverse children of color. In H. E. Fitzgerald, B. M. Lester, & B. S. Zuckerman (eds.), *Children of color: Research, health, and policy issues* (pp. 205–18). New York: Garland Publishing. https://doi.org/10.4324/9781315861302-10

McClelland, M. M., Geldhof, J. G., Cameron, C. E., & Wanless, S. B. (2015). Development and self-regulation. In W. F. Overton & P. C. Molenaar (eds.), *Theory and method. Handbook of child psychology and developmental science* (Vol 1, 1–43). Hoboken, NJ: Wiley. https://doi.org/10.1002/9781118963418.childpsy114

McCrae, R. R., Costa Jr, P. T. , Ostendorf, F., et al. (2000). Nature over nurture: Temperament, personality, and life span development. *Journal of Personality and Social Psychology, 78*(1), 173. https://doi.org/10.1037/0022-3514.78.1.173

McEwen, B. S. (2013). The brain on stress: Toward an integrative approach to brain, body, and behavior. *Perspectives on Psychological Science, 8*(6), 673–5. https://doi.org/10.1177/1745691613506907

McLoyd, V. C., Purtell, K. M., & Hardaway, C. R. (2015). Race, class, and ethnicity in young adulthood. In M. E. Lamb (eds.), *Socioemotional processes. Handbook of child psychology and developmental science* (Vol 3, 7th ed., pp. 366–418). Editor-in-chief: R. M. Lerner. Hoboken, NJ: Wiley. https://doi.org/10.1002/9781118963418.childpsy310

Meaney, M. (2010). Epigenetics and the biological definition of gene x environment interactions. *Child Development, 81*, 41–79. https://doi.org/10.1111/j.1467-8624.2009.01381.x

Misteli, T. (2013). The cell biology of genomes: Bringing the double helix to life. *Cell, 152*, 1209–12. https://doi.org/10.1016/j.cell.2013.02.048

Mistry, J. & Dutta, R. (2015). Human development and culture: Conceptual and methodological Issues. In W. F. Overton & P. C. Molenaar (eds.), *Theory and method. Handbook of child psychology and developmental science.* (Vol 1, 7th ed., pp. 369–406). Editor-in-chief: R. M. Lerner. Hoboken, NJ: Wiley. https://doi.org/10.1002/9781118963418.childpsy110

Molenaar, P. C. M. (2007). Psychological methodology will change profoundly due to the necessity to focus on intra-individual variation. *Integrative Psychological and Behavioral Science, 41*(1), 35–40. https://doi.org/10.1007/s12124-007-9011-1

Molenaar, P. C. M. (2013). On the necessity to use person-specific data analysis approaches in psychology. *European Journal of Developmental Psychology, 10*(1), 29–39. https://doi.org/10.1080/17405629.2012.747435

Molenaar, P. C. M. (2014). Dynamic models of biological pattern formation have surprising implications for understanding the epigenetics of development. *Research in Human Development, 11*, 50–62.

Molenaar, P. C. M. & Nesselroade, J. R. (2014). New trends in the inductive use of relational developmental systems theory: Ergodicity, nonstationarity, and heterogeneity. In P. C. Molenaar, R. M. Lerner, and K. M. Newell (eds.), *Handbook of developmental systems and methodology.* (pp. 442–62). New York: Guilford Press.

Molenaar, P. C. M. & Nesselroade, J. R. (2015). Systems methods for developmental research. In W. F. Overton & P. C. M. Molenaar (eds.), *Theory and method. Handbook of child psychology and developmental science* (Vol. 1, 7th ed., pp. 652–82). Editor-in-chief: R. M. Lerner. Hoboken, NJ: Wiley. https://doi.org/10.1002/9781118963418.childpsy117

Molenaar, P. C. M., Lerner, R. M., & Newell, K. (eds.) (2014). *Handbook of developmental systems theory and methodology.* New York: Guilford.

Moore, D. S. (2015). *The developing genome: An introduction to behavioral epigenetics.* New York: Oxford University Press. https://doi.org/10.1128/genomeA.00954-15

Murry, V. M., Butler-Barnes, S. T., Mayo-Gamble, T. L., & Inniss-Thompson, M. N. (2018). Excavating new constructs for family stress theories in the context of everyday life experiences of Black American families. *Journal of Family Theory & Review, 10*(2), 384–405.

Murry, V. M., Hill, N. E., Witherspoon, D., Berkel, C., & Bartz, D. (2015). Children in diverse social contexts. In M. H. Bornstein and T. Leventhal (eds.), *Ecological settings and processes.handbook of child psychology and developmental science* (Vol. 4, 7th ed., pp. 416–54). Editor-in-chief: R. M. Lerner. Hoboken, NJ: Wiley.

Nasir, N. (2012). *Racialized identities: Race and achievement for African-American youth.* Redwood City, CA: Stanford University Press. https://doi.org/10.1515/9780804779142

Nasir, N. S., Lee, C. D., Pea, R. & de Royston. M. M. (2020). *Handbook of the cultural foundations of learning.* New York: Routledge. https://doi.org/10.4324/9780203774977

Nasir, N. S., Warren, B., Rosebery, A., & Lee, C. (2014). Learning as a cultural process: Achieving equity through diversity. In K. Sawyer (ed.), *Cambridge handbook of the learning sciences* (2nd ed., pp. 489–504). New York: Cambridge University. https://doi.org/10.1017/CBO9780511816833.030

National Scientific Council on the Developing Child. (2004). Children's emotional development is built into the architecture of their brains. *Working Paper No. 2.* www.developingchild.harvard.edu

OCED. (2019). *PISA 2018 Results (Vol. 1): What students know and can do.* Paris: PISA, OCED Publishing. https://doi.org/10.1787/5f07c754-en

Okonofua, J. A., Walton, G. M., & Eberhardt, J. L. (2016). A vicious cycle: A social–psychological account of extreme racial disparities in school discipline. *Perspectives on Psychological Science, 11*(3), 381–98. https://doi.org/10.1177/1745691616635592

Osher, D., Cantor, P., Berg, J., Steyer, L. & Rose, T. (2020). Drivers of human development: How relationships and context shape learning and development. *Applied Developmental Science, 24*(1), 6–36. https://doi.org/10.1080/10888691.2017.1398650

Osher, D., Pittman, K., Young, J., et al. (2020). *Thriving, robust equity, and transformative learning & development: A more powerful conceptualization of the contributors to youth success.* Washington, DC: American Institutes for Research and Forum for Youth Investment.

Overton, W. F. (2015). Process and relational developmental systems. In W. F. Overton & P. C. M. Molenaar (eds.), *Theory and method. Handbook of child psychology and developmental science* (Vol 1, 7th ed., pp. 9–62).

Editor-in-chief: R. M. Lerner. Hoboken, NJ: Wiley. https://doi.org/10.1002 /9781118963418.childpsy102

Patel, J. A., Nielsen, F. B. H., Badiani, A. A., et al. (2020). Poverty, inequality and COVID-19: The forgotten vulnerable. *Public Health, 183*, 110–11. https://doi.org/10.1016/j.puhe.2020.05.006

Panofsky, A. (2014). *Misbehaving science: Controversy and the development of behavior genetics*. Chicago, IL: University of Chicago Press. https://doi.org /10.7208/chicago/9780226058597.001.0001

Payne, C. (1984) Multicultural education and racism in American schools. *Theory into Practice, 23*(2), 124–31. https://doi.org/10.1080 /00405848409543102

Perry, B. & Szalavitz, M. (2006). *The boy who was raised as a dog and other stories from a child psychiatrist's notebook: What traumatized children can teach us about loss, love, and healing*. New York: Basic Books.

Piaget, J. (1970). Piaget's theory. In P. H. Mussen (ed.), *Carmichael's manual of child psychology* (Vol. 1, 3rd ed., pp. 703–23). New York: Wiley.

Pigliucci, M. & Mueller, G. B. (2010). Elements of an extended evolutionary synthesis. In M. Pigliucci & G. B. Mueller (eds.), *Evolution – The extended synthesis* (pp. 3–17). Cambridge, MA: MIT Press. https://doi.org/10.7551 /mitpress/9780262513678.001.0001

Plomin, R. (2018). *Blueprint: How DNA makes us who we are*. Cambridge, MA: MIT Press and Allen Lane.

Post, R. M. & Weiss, S. R. B. (1997). Emergent properties of neural systems: How focal molecular neurobiological alterations can affect behavior. *Development and Psychopathology, 9*, 907–29.

Raeff, C. (2016). *Exploring the dynamics of human development: An integrative approach*. New York: Oxford University Press. https://doi.org/10.1093 /acprof:oso/9780199328413.001.0001

Ram, N. & Grimm, K. J. (2015). Growth curve modeling and longitudinal factor analysis. In W. F. Overton & P. C. M. Molenaar (eds.), *Theory and method. Handbook of child psychology and developmental science* (Vol 1, 7th ed., pp. 758–88). Editor-in-chief: R. M. Lerner. Hoboken, NJ: Wiley. https://doi.org /10.1002/9781118963418.childpsy120

Ram, N., Chow, S. M., Bowles, R. P., et al. (2005). Examining interindividual differences in cyclicity of pleasant and unpleasant affect using spectral analysis and item response modeling. *Psychometrika, 70*, 773–90. https://doi .org/10.1007/s11336-001-1270-5

Rhodes, J. E. (2020). *Older and wiser: New ideas for youth mentoring in the 21st century*. Cambridge, MA: Harvard University Press.

Richardson, K. (2017). *Genes, brains, and human potential: The science and ideology of human intelligence.* New York: Columbia University Press. https://doi.org/10.7312/rich17842

Rivas-Drake, D., Seaton, E. K., Markstrom, C., et al. (2014). Ethnic and Racial Identity in the 21st Century Study Group. Ethnic and racial identity in adolescence: Implications for psychosocial, academic, and health outcomes. *Child Development, 85*(1), 40–57.

Rogoff, B. (2003). *The cultural nature of human development.* New York: Oxford University Press.

Rose, H. & Rose, S. (eds.). (2000). *Alas poor Darwin: Arguments against evolutionary psychology.* London: Vintage.

Rose, T. (2016). *The end of average: How we succeed in a world that values sameness.* New York: HarperCollins Publishers. https://doi.org/10.1007/s12020-016-0866-0

Rose, L. T., Rouhani, P., & Fischer, K. W. (2013). The science of the individual. *Mind, Brain, and Education, 7*(3), 152–58. https://doi.org/10.1111/mbe.12021

Rowan-Kenyon, H. T. , Martínez Alemán, A. M, & Savitz-Romer, M. (2018). *Technology and engagement: Making technology work for first generation college students.* New Brunswick, NJ: Rutgers University Press.

Rushton, J. P. (2000). *Race, evolution, and behavior* (2nd special abridged ed.). New Brunswick, NJ: Transaction Publishers.

Sampson, R. J. (2016). The characterological imperative: On Heckman, Humphries, and Kautz's *The myth of achievement tests: The GED and the role of character in American Life. Journal of Economic Literature, 54*(2), 493–513. https://doi.org/10.1257/jel.54.2.493

Schore, A. M. (2016). *Affect regulation and the origin of the self: The neuro-biology of emotional development.* New York: Routledge. https://doi.org/10.4324/9781315680019

Shonkoff, J. P. (2017). *Building a system for science-based R&D that achieves breakthrough outcomes at scale for young children facing adversity.* Cambridge, MA: Center on the Developing Child, Harvard University.

Siegel, D. J. (2020). *The developing mind: How relationships and the brain interact to shape who we are* (3rd ed.). New York: Guilford. https://doi.org/10.1093/mind/fzz082

Slavich, G. M. (2020). Social safety theory: A biologically based evolutionary perspective on life stress, health, and behavior. *Annual Review of Clinical Psychology, 16,* 256–95. https://doi.org/10.1146/annurev-clinpsy-032816-045159

Slavich, G. M. & Cole, S. W. (2013). The emerging field of human social genomics. *Clinical Psychological Science, 1*, 331–48. https://doi.org/10 .1177/2167702613478594

Spencer, M. B. (2006). Phenomenological variant of ecological systems theory (PVEST): A human development synthesis applicable to diverse individuals and groups. In W. Damon & R.M. Lerner (eds.) & R. M. Lerner (Vol. ed.), *Theoretical models of human development. Handbook of child psychology* (Vol. 6, 6th ed., pp. 829–94). Hoboken, NJ: Wiley.

Spencer, M. B. (2008). Phenomenology and ecological systems theory: Development of diverse groups. In W. Damon and R. M. Lerner (eds.), *Child and adolescent development: An advanced course* (pp. 696–735). New York: Wiley Publishers. https://doi.org/10.1002/9780470147658 .chpsy0115

Spencer, M. B. & Spencer, T. R. (2014). Exploring the promises, intricacies, and challenges to Positive Youth Development. *Journal of Youth and Adolescence, 43*, 1027–35.

Spencer, M. B., Swanson, D. P., & Harpalani, V. (2015). Development of the self. In M. E. Lamb (Vol. ed.), *Socioemotional processes. Handbook of child psychology and developmental science* (Vol. 3, 7th ed., pp. 750–93). Editor-in -chief: R. M. Lerner.

Stafford-Brizard, B. (2016). *Building blocks for learning: A framework for comprehensive student development*. New York: Turnaround for Children.

Steenbeek, H. & van Geert, P. (2020). Education and development as complex dynamic agent systems. In M. F. Mascolo & T. R. Bidell (eds.), *Handbook of integrative developmental science: Essays in honor of Kurt W. Fischer* (pp. 162–88). New York: Routledge. https://doi.org/10.4324 /9781003018599-6

Takaki, R. (2012). *A different mirror: A history of multicultural America* (Revised ed.). New York: Back Bay Books/Little, Brown and Company.

Thelen, E. & Smith, L. B. (2006). Dynamic systems theories. In R. M. Lerner & W. Damon (eds.), *Handbook of child psychology. Theoretical models of human development* (Vol. 1, 6th ed., pp. 258–312). Hoboken, NJ: John Wiley & Sons, Inc.

Theokas, C. & Lerner, R. M. (2006). Observed ecological assets in families, schools, and neighborhoods: Conceptualization, measurement, and relations with positive and negative developmental outcomes. *Applied Developmental Science, 10*(2), 61–74. https://doi.org/10.1207/s1532480xads1002_2

Tobach, E. & Schneirla, T. C. (1968). The biopsychology of social behavior of animals. In R. E. Cooke & S. Levin (eds.), *Biologic basis of pediatric practice* (pp. 68–82). New York: McGraw-Hill.

Tucker, M. S. (2020a). *Race in America 2020*. NCCE, June 18. https://ncee.org/2020/06/race-in-america-2020/

Tucker, M. S. (2020b). *COVID-19 and our schools: The real challenge*. NCCE, June 26. https://ncee.org/2020/06/covid-19-and-our-schools-the-real-challenge/

Umaña-Taylor, A. J., Douglass, S., Updegraff, K. A., & Marsiglia, F. F. (2018). A small-scale randomized efficacy trial of the Identity Project: Promoting adolescents' ethnic–racial identity exploration and resolution. *Child Development*, *89*(3), 862–70.

von Bertalanffy, L. (1933). *Modern theories of development*. London: Oxford University Press.

von Eye, A., Bergman, L. R., & Hsieh, C. A. (2015). Person-oriented methodological approaches. In W. F. Overton & P. C. M. Molenaar (eds.), *Theory and method. Handbook of child psychology and developmental science* (Vol 1, 7th ed., pp. 789–841). Hoboken, NJ: Wiley. https://doi.org/10.1002/9781118963418.childpsy121

Vygotsky, L. (1978). *Mind in society: The development of higher psychological processes* (M. Cole, V. John-Steiner, S. Scribner, & E. Souberman, Trans.). Cambridge, MA: Harvard University Press.

Werner, H. (1948). *Comparative psychology of mental development*. New York: International Universities Press.

Werner, H. & Kaplan, B. (1963). *Symbol formation: An organismic-developmental approach to language and the expression of thought*. New York: Wiley.

Wilkerson, I. (2020). *Caste: The origins of our discontents*. New York: Random House Publishing Group.

Winthrop, R. (2018). *Leapfrogging inequality: Remaking education to help young people thrive*. Washington, DC: The Brookings Institution.

West-Eberhard, M. J. (2003). *Developmental plasticity and evolution*. New York: Oxford University Press. https://doi.org/10.1093/oso/9780195122343.001.0001

Yu, D., Yang, P-J., Geldhof, J., et al. (2020). Exploring idiographic approaches to children's executive function performance: An intensive longitudinal study. *Journal for Person Oriented Research*, *6*(2), 73–87. https://doi.org/10.17505/jpor.2020.22401

Zelazo, P. D., Anderson, J. E., Richler, J., et al. (2013). II. NIH toolbox cognition battery (CB): Measuring executive function and attention. *Monographs of the Society for Research in Child Development*, *78*(4), 16–33. https://doi.org/10.1111/mono.12032

Zukav, G. (1979). *The dancing Wu Li masters*. New York: Bantam.

Cambridge Elements ≡

Child Development

Marc H. Bornstein
National Institute of Child Health and Human Development, Bethesda
Institute for Fiscal Studies, London
UNICEF, New York City
Marc H. Bornstein is an Affiliate of the *Eunice Kennedy Shriver* National Institute of Child Health and Human Development, an International Research Fellow at the Institute for Fiscal Studies (London), and UNICEF Senior Advisor for Research for ECD Parenting Programmes. Bornstein is President Emeritus of the Society for Research in Child Development, Editor Emeritus of *Child Development*, and founding Editor of *Parenting: Science and Practice*.

About the Series
Child development is a lively and engaging, yet serious and purposeful subject of academic study that encompasses myriad of theories, methods, substantive areas, and applied concerns. Cambridge Elements in Child Development proposes to address all these key areas, with unique, comprehensive, and state-of-the-art treatments, introducing readers to the primary currents of research and to original perspectives on, or contributions to, principal issues and domains in the field.

Cambridge Elements $\equiv$

Child Development

Elements in the Series

A full series listing is available at: www.cambridge.org/EICD